FINDING YOUR MORE

REBECCA PLATT

Published by HENDRICK NORTON, 2023.

While every precaution has been taken in the preparation of this book, the publisher assumes no responsibility for errors or omissions, or for damages resulting from the use of the information contained herein.

FINDING YOUR MORE

First edition. December 23, 2023.

ISBN: 979-8223762065

Written by REBECCA PLATT.

Also by REBECCA PLATT

Depression Has a Big Voice. Make Yours Bigger!
FINDING YOUR MORE
Deeper

Watch for more at https://goodthoughtsgoodlives.com.

Table of Contents

AUTHOR'S NOTES

Well, another one bites the dust, and I feel like I'm about to because this was a challenging book to write.

My first book was as well, but I had, more or less, written it years before. I had tons of material from retreats and conferences I spoke at. I had lots of Bible note from classes I taught. My notes from my Clinical Pastor Education training assignments were also a source. So, it was more of a matter of putting it all together. I had already done the reading and the research.

I started this book from a blank page and might add a blank brain.

But from the beginning, I had the book's concept and title in my head. I never rethought the idea because I loved the concept of "more" from the start. It seemed to me that God's word is clear about how much more he wants for each of us. I think many people don't believe God has singled them out for anything. I hope to dispel this month.

As I reread the stories of these people you will meet in this book, I still find myself at how God used them, despite their shortcomings and even despite their successes. God can lift up anyone for his purpose and he can bring someone low if that's what is needed.

This book required tons of Bible research, which I love anyway, so that was a win-win for me. The idea of' "more" fascinated me because it implies that there is always something beyond our current limitations, urging us to reach further and strive for extraordinary achievements. I delved into the rich tapestry of the men and women in the Bible and their stories. They became "friends."

A couple of editing notes. I decided not to capitalize He, Him, His unless it occurred at the beginning of a sentence or in scripture. Some authors do, and some don't. Max Lucado doesn't, but Andy Stanley does. I find it easier to read without capitalization. Also, I didn't italicize scripture verses unless it was dialogue. Again, there are no rules here.

Thanks to my husband for seeing me through this one as well. I'm only just beginning. Follow my blog at www.goodthoughtsgoodlives.com[1] for the latest updates on new books. I also contribute regularly to FB, IG, Tumblr, and LinkedIn.

I give God the glory for the idea and the words of this book. I hope you find it helpful.

GOD BLESS

---

1. http://www.goodthoughtsgoodlives.com

ONE: WHAT IS A MORE

- What is a more?

- Who has a more?

- Could I already be living my more?

- Why do I need a more?

- What is the time frame for my more?

- Is finding your more the answer to everything?

And why am I making an adjective a noun?

I will give you some quick answers so you understand my premises for this book, but all the above questions are discussed in more detail in various sections.

More is more.

More is knowing what God has called you to do, that specific assignment that only you can do and that fulfills God's plan and purpose for you. Others will have their versions of their more, but only you can have yours. Like you, each more is unique.

Everyone has a more. God created you on purpose and for a purpose. You are not the only one he forgot. You have a more. You have a mission, a purpose, a calling. There are no exceptions.

Could you already be living your more? Of course. You may have already done all the soul-searching I suggest in this book and have realized you are doing precisely what God has called you to do in this season of your life. I will share with you my personal story that makes this point.

Is there a daily more? Yes and no.

Surely, we all know there is always more we can do to further God's kingdom, so in that case, it's yes. But it probably does mean that every day, once you know your more, you are stepping closer to fulfilling that more as you study, pray, and think.

Your more, however, will not necessarily be practiced every day. For example, my more, writing, means my gifts of encouragement and teaching are fulfilled when my books are finished and in the hands of readers. That doesn't mean I shouldn't look daily for other ways to use them. The other day, I asked God, "How can I use my gifts today?" It should always be simmering in the back of our minds.

Everyone needs a more.

Why do I say everyone needs a more? Well, it isn't just me that says it. It's God.

Over and over again God's word, we are encouraged to heed God's more, his call on our lives. Back to the very first point. He created you on purpose for a purpose. It is clear from reading scripture that we are fulfilled and lead happier and more content lives following God's unique plan for us. So, you need to know your more for your personal well-being.

Is more the answer to everything? In other words, will you be blissfully happy and content with no struggles? Of course not. But will you be more contented and better able to manage your struggles?

Yes. Because there is something about knowing you are doing what you are supposed to do that brings such a calming peace of mind.

And why in the world am I using an adjective as a noun? For that, you will have to read further. But the quick answer is that I like the word better than purpose, calling, and mission. Although, as I will point out, you *can* substitute those words if you want.

I mentioned the title of this book to a friend, and it intrigued her. She loved the whole concept of more and said, "That's interesting; I want to give that some thought. I've never thought of God's plan for my life as a more". That was encouraging to me. I hope you find it encouraging as well.

Everyone has a more.

We find our more by living our lives, by putting one God-directed foot in front of the other.

Mores aren't static, though. They change with the seasons of our lives. Our mores grow and develop as we do. Mores run the gamut, as you will learn in this book.

- Sometimes, they are so big that we are overwhelmed.
- Sometimes, they are small and quiet.
- Sometimes, we find our more but must put it on a shelf, not to be forgotten but to simmer for a time. We might need to learn new skills, or circumstances may need to change.
- But all mores fit under the umbrella of the spiritual gifts God gave each of us at our spiritual rebirth. Any activity or interest outside our spiritual gifts might be perfectly OK to pursue, but they are not our spiritual gifts.

More is one hundred percent scriptural. Find a verse in Scripture that says we should ever want less. To *have or possess less*, maybe, to covet less, absolutely, but never to *experience* less.

The verse that prompted this book is:

"Now to him who can do immeasurably more than all we ask or imagine, according to his power that is at work within us." *(Ephesians 3:20) NASB* *All following Scripture verses are taken from the NASB unless otherwise noted.)

The synonyms from Strong's Concordance for the word "more" are exceeding and abundant. In other words, more. Our more depends on the leading of the Holy Spirit because, again, that's what the verse states.

I could have classified the mores in many ways, but I arbitrarily chose ten classifications based on reading the stories of the great heroes *and* the not-so-great ones in the Bible. I also chose the examples I did because they spoke to me the most.

You may find that pairing certain people with specific categories is not what you would have chosen had you written this book. That's OK. Feel free to disagree. I tried to look at each person's overall life when I placed them where I did, and sometimes, they could easily have been included in more than one category. Some examples are only snapshots in time-based on one incident.

I read and reread the stories of men and women in scripture and how their more played out in their lives. These men and women became almost real as I tried to step into their stories, sometimes with very little information. I imagined how they felt without putting too much of myself into their stories.

I omitted substantial amounts from some longer stories but

tried to stay true to the overall substance and meaning. I made some assumptions based on my educational background in Psychology, Clinical Pastoral Education, hospital chaplaincy experience, and my knowledge of scripture.

Who has a more?

Again, we all have a more. When we were just a thought in God's mind, he already planned our future. It has been with us and part of us since our birth. We are fearfully and wonderfully made; part of that wonder is our calling. You can no more deny it than you can your name.

It's not hidden. It lies within you, waiting for you to discover it. And it's not like you have to work for it or dig for it. It's not elusive. As you learn to recognize God's voice, the closer your walk to God becomes, the closer you are to recognizing it and living your more.

"I know the plans I have for you, declares LORD, plans for prosperity and not for disaster, to give you a hope and a future." This message was for the Israelites living in captivity under King Nebuchadnezzar's rule. They had been listening to false prophets instead of to God. Someone else was telling them what their more was. God makes it clear in this passage that only he makes plans for his people, "I know the plans *I* have for you."

The time frame for your more

So, what is the time frame? Meaning, is your more an everyday thing? Is it every few weeks, months, or years? Your more lives within all those time frames.

It might take months or years to set your more in motion. Depending on the complexity and degree of training required, your more might require additional training or certain circumstances may have to be in place. But then again, today might be the day. There are no set parameters. My mores of encouragement and teaching took on many forms at various stages of my life. It wasn't until ten years ago that it morphed into writing and blogging.

Once you know your more, you will probably find it takes various forms, just like life. It will be a process, and there will be times when it could be fulfilled daily. Other times, like many of my examples, it might be for a particular season or reason. And once that season or reason has expired, so has that version of your more.

There are no set rules regarding when this pursuit should begin; it could start any day. The concept of "more" is described as something that can change and evolve, much like life itself. Fulfilling one's "more" is seen as a process that may have periods of daily fulfillment or might be more relevant during specific seasons or for particular reasons. Once you know your spiritual gifts, your more will fall into place.

We are to follow God's revealed will as he has made it known to all Christians through his word. We are to be seeking his daily will for us through prayer. But your more is beyond the general will of God. This book will help you discover and pursue your more.

TWO: WHY DO I NEED A MORE?

There are four reasons why finding your more is essential. They are:

- Fulfillment
- Direction
- Balance
- Relevance

Fulfillment

Have you ever been afraid to tackle something? How did you feel when you did, and it worked?

You felt great, didn't you? You had accomplished something, and you felt proud. At the end of a long day, you looked back over your day and thought, "Wow, I feel good about what I did." Finding your more and living your more brings a deep sense of fulfillment that permeates your being. It's more than just fleeting happiness; it's a lasting contentment that comes from aligning your actions with your values and goals in keeping with God's revelation of his more for you.

This feeling of "all is right with my world" emanates from a combination of accomplishment, peace, and purpose. It's like a puzzle piece clicking into place, completing a picture that represents your true self. This profound satisfaction fills you spiritually and emotionally, leaving you feeling whole and fulfilled. Discovering and embracing your more leads to a harmonious balance and a profound sense of well-being that transcends mere satisfaction.

While it's good to pursue enjoyable activities, the ultimate contentment and direction in life stem from the belief that one is fulfilling a specific plan, in this case, referred to as more. Our more provides clarity and purpose to our existence.

I felt discouraged during a period in my life because it seemed I was giving too much of myself compared to what I was getting in return. I was having a pity party. Our more comes from God and thus should not be subject to emotional ups and downs. Once I remember this giving of myself was one of the ways I fulfill my more, encouragement, I immediately felt much lighter in my spirit. I reframed my perspective to one of outward gratification as opposed to self-gratification.

Why?

Because I realized I didn't have to worry about the return on my investment. I didn't have to look to other people to bolster me up. I only had an audience of one, and that made all the difference. We forget that God is the one who sees our efforts, and he is the one to whom we are responsible. If you seek to live out your more for the appreciation you will receive, think again.

A reason to discover your personal more is that once you do, you will find yourself less likely to look to others for approval as I had done. You will know you are doing exactly what God has called you to do. So, if you find some of this difficult to implement, you are in good company. I literally wrote the book, and I still find it challenging to live out my more like I should. I, too, fall into the trap of living some of my days without purposeful direction. I know that writing is what I should be doing, but there are days I want to do everything but. I have to remind myself that writing is my more, my purpose, and I always feel better when I'm in the flow of fulfilling it. Even today, though, I feel an overwhelming need to spray paint something.

Direction

Living out our more brings direction to your day. It makes it easy to decide what you will or will not do (like spray painting something) and helps you with time management. I was on the first edit of this book, trying to get some posts ready for my blog, packing to head to the cabin, getting a few DIYs done for the blog, etc. As I thought about what I was doing, I asked myself, "Which of these activities brings me closer to meeting my goal of getting this first edit done?" I realized two things had to change.

First was my blogging schedule. I couldn't keep blogging three or four days a week and still accomplish my goal, so I changed from posting three days to two until this book was done. Besides, it was summer, and I figured most people didn't want e-mail flooding their inboxes. So that decision was easy. (Earlier in the year, I quit following all my favorite blogs and instead made a list of them in the back of my journal. When I have the time, I pick one or two and see what's new. That made a huge difference. Social media is one of the biggest stumbling blocks in fulfilling your more.)

The second issue was the DIY part of my blog. The blog title was faithsighanddiy. I realized that while I love doing DIY projects, it was too time-consuming. Plus, my photography skills were minimal. I decided to leave that part of blogging to the "influencers."

Then I realized that no one even knew what "sigh" meant in the title. (By the way, it refers to mental health. Sighing is a common symptom of depression and anxiety.)

That part of my blog had to go, too. But then that posted a problem with the name of the blog. I contacted my hosting site and found I could change my domain name without deleting my original name, thus redirecting my followers. So, I changed the name to goodthoughtsgoodlives.com.

Do you see how these decisions directly resulted from knowing what God called me to do and how I was able to center everything else around that? When you know your purpose, it provides a clear direction for your life.

Balance

Knowing our more keeps the scales of our lives better balanced. Back to my illustration. I find my life is far more balanced now that I've identified my more. It also helped me realize that I'm only one person. And one person can't meet everyone's needs. We can pray about those needs and do what we can. But we can't solve everyone's issues. (I could write another book about that, couldn't I? It's a problem many of us knights-on-a-white-horse have in common.) As long as we can think we can take care of everyone's needs, it will be almost impossible to find and fulfill our mores.

Knowing our more keeps all this in balance because we see what we need to do, making it easier to let go of the things we don't need to do. I am not suggesting things will always run on an even keel just because you know your more, but I do suggest that it will bring your life back into balance when it's all askew. Your focus won't be so all-over-the-place chaotic. Let me explain further.

An all-over-the-place chaotic life is a life where things pop around us, like those toy vacuum cleaners of a few years ago. You know the ones. When the child pushes it, the balls jump around, to the child's delight. They think they are vacuuming like their parents.

I know way too many people who live lives like this. Their lives jump all over the place and are substantially out of whack. Here's the thing though:

- We can read good books about organization.
- We can buy storage bins.
- We can label everything.
- We can have our daily planners up-to-date and our tasks marked off our list.

That's all good. I enjoy living like that. I like to be organized. I function so much better. But all that organizing doesn't mean you are living a balanced life. It only means you are living an organized life—big difference.

Picture those scales again. Your more is on one side, and everything else is on the other. At times, of course, the "everything else" might weigh its side down because of life's demands. However, knowing your more helps you recognize it immediately and make the needed corrections.

I recently had my own experience with an out-of-balance life.

Mine.

My husband and I were finishing our first week of the 2022 summer at our cabin. We were already two months behind due to weather and a stalled pump installation. It was a nightmare week. A new submersible pump, and count them, one, two, three, serious water leaks after the pump installation. (New pump + old pipes = leaks.) That meant removing the flashing that goes around the bottom of the cabin. It meant digging holes in the rain. It meant trying to be nice to each other.

There's more. (No, not that one.) We keep an old truck at the cabin during the summer, so when my husband goes fishing for the day, I have an available vehicle in case I want to go somewhere. The brakes went out the same week.

Then we came home and discovered we needed to replace the upstairs toilet and the downstairs shower head.

I had planned on getting a lot of writing and editing done that week at the cabin, and none of that happened. We did what we had to do. Things were out of balance because that's life, but knowing my more got me back on track despite it all. Besides,

I'm always somewhat grateful, after the fact, of course, when these annoyances happen because I am reminded that life is unpredictable at best but that God is not.

Relevance

Finally, our more bring relevance. Relevance isn't something we read about often, yet it's a significant issue for many people. There's something about naming our more that brings relevance. When we realize we have a role to play in God's kingdom, something God has asked us to do, we feel part of something bigger. We feel significant. We feel relevant.

And that's because we are.

While we were always significant in God's eyes, now we see it ourselves and feel a little pumped about it. It feels fantastic. There's nothing wrong with feeling good because we know we are living out God's plan for our lives. Why shouldn't we?

Everyone wants to feel relevant. It can be challenging for people at the opposite ends of the age spectrum. On the one hand, we're too young, so what do we know? On the other hand, we're too old, so what do we know? But *everyone* is relevant in God's plan and has a significant role.

You and your more are relevant. For this not to be true would mean that God didn't create you *on* purpose and *for* a purpose. It would be to deny what God's word says. When we lose our sense of purpose, we lose our zest for living. Many senior citizens struggle with this. They feel their opinions are no longer important. No one asks what they think about significant issues anymore. I've had some of my most meaningful conversations with those who are young and those who are old. Somehow, the truth seems to flow more easily and gently with people at each end of life's spectrum.

Everyone needs to feel relevant, but so many don't. So, smile at people more often. Say hello. If you need a more, there's one God may have for you, making people feel relevant. And a simple "Hello" can accomplish that. Lives can be changed when people know others "see" them. Hagar's prayer in Genesis 16: 1-14 is a good example. Being 'seen' is important. The most significant mores might be the simplest.

Why am I making an adjective a noun?

I chose the title "Finding Your More" because finding one's more is a process, except for thrust-upon-mores, which you will read about. For some, the journey was long. Some threw away their more. Some threw away their mores. Some detoured from their mores, and some never found it.

I wanted this book's title to raise eyebrows and bring questions to mind. I could've used the word 'purpose' because a more is a purpose, but it is also so much more. (See the play on words there?) Besides, the word 'purpose' sounds very academic and intimidating. Not everyone will want a purpose, but who doesn't want more?

The word more immediately implies a dream, a vision, something we are enthusiastic about. Many Christians already know their more; they've been down the road of prayer and self-reflection and discovered their calling. Some Christians are completely satisfied with their status quo and don't need this challenge. Others are still searching. For others, finding their purpose is a new concept. Wherever you land, you will find this book helpful.

I am using the word "more" as a noun, although I will also use it as it's commonly used. This use of the word will take some getting used to. I also chose not always to italicize or put the word in quotation marks every time, as I felt this would annoy and distract the reader. It certainly would me. So envision those quotation marks in your head when you read the word. No matter how I tried to come up with another title or word to use, I kept coming back to "more."

You can substitute passion, purpose, or call if you have to. I won't be offended.

Is finding your more the answer to everything?

- Will you be happier?
- Will your relationships be better?
- Will you struggle less?

Anytime we are genuinely at peace with God and ourselves, all parts of our lives improve. But happiness doesn't compare to the immeasurable peace (Philippians 4:7) you experience when you follow God's more for your life. What could bring more happiness anyway than knowing you are doing *exactly* what God created you to do? I find happiness highly overrated.

Happiness usually depends on circumstance, while peace doesn't. We can find peace amid the crisis because God is the source of that peace, not circumstances.

A Christian who knows and pursues their more is likely to have healthier relationships, too. That's because we are taking our preoccupation with ourselves and redirecting it. Knowing our more takes the focus off ourselves. Thank goodness. Right?

The struggling part I can answer by pointing to Charles Spurgeon, the Prince of Preachers. Most people don't know that Spurgeon suffered his entire life from depression and spent months in bed at a time. And if ever there was someone who found his more and was using it to the fullest, it was Spurgeon. So, will you struggle less once you embrace your more? If we could ask Charles Spurgeon whether his calling made a difference in his battle with depression, what do you think he would have said? I think he would say it made **all** the difference.

People haven't changed.

"All have sinned." Human nature hasn't changed since Adam and Eve were ejected from the garden. Most of us think of Biblical characters very narrowly because we have little information about them. And because they *are* in the Bible, we assume it's because they were near-perfect people.

Hardly.

They felt love, anger, hurt, guilt, joy, etc., just like we do. God used very flawed people (a few exceptions) as teaching examples because we, too, are very flawed and thus can relate. But even for those that appear near perfect, we know they weren't.

Moses was headstrong. Solomon was prideful. David was easily tempted. Peter was a hot head. Nathanial was a doubter. Martha was, well, Martha. These are just a few examples of the many flawed people God used.

There are no new sins.

Think if you were trying to write your entire life history, including your thoughts. And what if you had to condense it into a few pages like it is for most people in the Bible? You wouldn't be able to do it. Therefore, much of what we surmise about these people is from their actions.

"Actions speak louder than words" was as true back then as it is today. So, that's what I did. I looked at their actions and based on what I learned about the individual and what I know about human nature, I made some well-thought-out conclusions.

People can use many words, but most of us look more at what people do than what they say. It's the most authentic barometer of a person's life. For example, I can tell people I'm a loving person, but if my actions don't show it, "I am a noisy gong or a clanging cymbal." (I Corinthians 13: 1.) In other words, it's not true. As you will learn, the apostle Peter always proclaimed his undying allegiance to Jesus. Yet, his actions sometimes indicated something else.

THREE: AN OVERVIEW

First, do no harm.

I kept thinking about this book within those parameters. It percolated in my head like the coffee pots of old gurgling on the stove. I struggled with how to write a book like this and remembered the oath doctors take: "First, do no harm." What do I mean by that?

Sometimes, books like this cause us to question ourselves ad infinitum. "Oh, no, what if I'm not fulfilling my more"? Or "What if I never find my more?" Or the worst, "What if I've thrown away my more, and it's too late?"

You can read a book like this and get discouraged. You end up feeling you're a big disappointment to God. Worse, maybe you think you're too much this or not enough that to even have a more. Or you are too little *this* or too little *that*.

But then you might go the other way and say, "Well, I'm just fine where I am; thank you very much." And that's OK, too. We are all in different maturing stages.

This book helps you identify *your* more. Some of you may be there right now. For now. Your more changes as the seasons of your life change. Young couples with little children and full-time jobs are in a much different place than empty nesters. The expression of our more looks different in those two scenarios. That makes perfect sense.

The spiritual gifts umbrella

While your more will change as your season changes, it will always fall under the umbrella of your spiritual gifts.

I know a young woman who has the gift of encouragement. She has a full-time job and two boys, one with special needs. She expresses her more through little acts of kindness and generosity to her family, neighbors, and employees. She doesn't have much time for activities requiring more involvement.

She leaves small gift cards for Starbucks, where she assumes they will be found, keeps lunch bags in her car to give to the homeless she sees on the street corner, and volunteers at her church. Her more is limited to the activities she has time for now. Her gift of encouragement will probably look very different ten years from now when her children are adults.

When I was her age, mine looked different, too. But now, I have the time to devote to writing and blogging, which fall under the umbrella of my spiritual gifts: teaching and encouraging. And speaking of spiritual gifts.

God disperses spiritual gifts to everyone. Often, they are in line with your natural talents and abilities, although those may yet be discovered. He created you with specific talents and abilities when you were born. Why would he then give you a spiritual gift outside those parameters?

Of course, some Christians believe they have no special gift. The Bible says otherwise. You may not have uncovered yours yet, and it may take being thrown in water over your head before you do, but you are not the exception. You are gifted, and God has given you a specific way (your more) to express your spiritual gift.

Some of you may stop right here because you don't know your spiritual gift. This book will not address the spiritual gifts, but there are good sources I will provide later in the book. Within those categories, there are myriad variations and possibilities.

But I can't think of any more that wouldn't fit somewhere under one of the general gifts. Some Bible references are Romans 12:6-8, I Corinthians 12, and Ephesians 4:11.

For example, the gift of encouragement could include hundreds of professions and outlets, as could the gift of teaching. Don't limit your thinking, and don't raise an eyebrow if God leads you to express yours unconventionally.

It isn't complicated.

Knowing your spiritual gifts isn't that complicated. There are tests you can take, books you can read, and other complex resources. If that's your thing, go ahead. Otherwise, simple questions you can ask yourself will steer you in the right direction.

- What do I love to do?
- What do I hate to do?
- What are you naturally good at? (Trust me, there are many.)
- What makes me excited to get up in the morning?

- What books do I like to read?
- What movies do I like to watch?
- What stories in the Bible ring my chimes?

These will jumpstart your thinking, and when you read about the gifts, certain ones will stand out. It will all fall into place, and you will know your general category. From there, anything is possible. A good source for learning about your gifts is www./chazwon.com. Chazwon is the Hebrew word for vision. "And with no vision, no awareness of our purpose for living, our inner life shrivels up and dies." Craig Groeschel, author of *Chazwon.*

Just like my more, the expression of yours will be highly individualized. I've known mine for a long time. My more has always been under the umbrella of encouragement and teaching. Yours will fall under your spiritual gifts umbrella as well.

I talked to someone about this concept more while working on this introduction. You know how it is when something nags at you, like a hair in your eyes. You keep flicking it away, and you can't figure out where it's coming from, and it's driving you up the wall, and you are getting annoyed? Like that.

Anyway, I had this discussion with a good friend. This woman is a gentle, beautiful soul. She represents that reader I mentioned earlier, who I feared would feel guilty if I did a poor job explaining this concept. She is not one of those out-there, extroverted kinds of people. When she thinks of purposes and missions, she thinks, as do many, that this is for public ministries, such as pastors, missionaries, Bible teachers, and so on. And, of course, it isn't. We started talking about this concept of more. Stay with me here because this is good if I say so myself.

She expressed sadness because she felt she didn't have a purpose or a mission. (Didn't I say I was worried this book would do that? Well, this was proving to be my first test case.) We threw around some ideas, and I tried to clarify what I was saying but wasn't doing very well. Then she mentioned her neighbors.

New neighbors have moved in on each side of her. She had already befriended her neighbors anyway because that's who she is. Still, once we discussed it, she identified this activity as her more. I wish you could have seen her expression when she realized she did have a more. She didn't realize being a friend to a neighbor could be a more.

I talked to her the next day; she had already introduced herself and offered to help her neighbors with whatever they needed. I could tell she was excited.

Now, I know what you're thinking. "Rebecca, wasn't your friend going to do those things, anyway?"

Yes, yes, she was. But here's what made the difference.

Naming your more.

Once she labeled her more as hospitality, she made it her mission. She felt commissioned. She became intentional about it. It's a place where she can hang her hat because she gave it a name. And it sparked her imagination.

Imagination is an attribute Christians don't generally think about when they think of faith. But God is the creator of our imagination. All one has to do is look at nature. No one but a creator with a vast imagination could have come up with everything we see in nature every day. Thinking about our more can prompt our imagination, which might well give us more insight.

I went snorkeling once, and if anyone had told me such beauty existed beneath the water's surface, I wouldn't have believed them. I still remember how I felt when I saw the coral and the tropical fish. Now, that's an imaginative God! Watch some Planet Earth episodes to see just how much imagination God has. They also show God has a great sense of humor. He has created some pretty funny-looking creatures. Nature is more, is it not?

Since I wrote this, my friend still considers befriending her neighbors as her more. She has since taken it to a new level because she can now see various ways to express her more. And all because she now sees it as her commission, her unique purpose.

Let me take this further.

I call myself a writer. I didn't use to call myself a writer, even after I published my first book. I knew writing was my more, but once I gave it a name, it became my identity, who I am, and my personal more. The simple fact of giving it a name gave me the desire to write the second book.

Naming something makes it concrete. And once you name your more, there is a level of accountability. It keeps you intentional.

So, in learning our more, or if you already know yours, naming it spurs us on. Our more becomes who we are, our identity. And that makes accomplishing our more so much easier. We are renewed. "Therefore, if anyone is in Christ, he is a new creation; the old things have passed away, behold, new things have come." (2 Corinthians 5:17)

That young woman I mentioned with the two boys and a full-time job? Once we talked and she identified that her spiritual gift was encouragement, it became her identity. That opened up her thinking about the many ways she could express it within her current time restrictions. Knowing our spiritual gift opens the way to recognizing our more.

What we call ourselves and how we identify ourselves put us on the right path. Words matter especially the words we speak to ourselves.

We all know that is true. If we call ourselves victims, we remain victims. If we call ourselves overcomers, we become overcomers. We often live our lives based on the identity we have chosen for ourselves. We do it to other people, too. Call someone a loser, and he will continue to make decisions that keep him a loser.

Now, when I sit down to write, I take myself and my new identity seriously. I am a writer. The more I say it, the less strange it sounds and the more it defines me. I set up my workspace to reinforce that I'm indeed a writer. Identifying my personal more and changing what I called myself made a big difference.

When we clearly understand what God calls us to do in a particular season of our lives, we look at ourselves differently. We now wake up with a sense of purpose and anticipation because we know our more.

The journey begins

I wrote this book for those willing to take this journey, even those who think it isn't for them. You may feel you have missed or screwed up your more, and now it's too late. I've got that covered. You may feel you aren't worthy of a more. Covered. What if you threw it away? Covered. I will cover a lot.

And, by the way, I felt all those ways myself.

Identifying our more and naming it makes a difference. The problem is that too many of us haven't even searched for it. And if we aren't seeking our more, or at least have identified our more, we are merely settling. God has a more for you, and you will find it. This book will help.

Our more is not static. It's not like you find your more, and that's it; there's nothing more to be done.

There might even be a period when your more is multi-dimensional. For many months, my more was writing only. Now, I focus on marketing the first book and writing this one. So, I have a *process* more and an *outcome* more going on simultaneously. As in any project, there are various fronts to address simultaneously.

Also, there might be a long preparation period before our more comes to fruition. Moses spent forty years in the desert as God prepared him for his more. The apostle Paul spent three years in Arabia. Jesus spent thirty years in preparation.

In the book of Colossians, Paul coins a beautiful phrase, "perfect patience." That's what God has: perfect patience (I Timothy 1:16). God works in his perfectly patient time to bring our more to fruition. But just as God expresses perfect patience, we must practice our patience as we take this journey of self-discovery.

A sense of unfulfillment is often evidence that there is a more for us. We feel like we are sleepwalking through our faith. Have you ever felt that way? I certainly have. Sometimes, I felt like I was giving my faith lip service. Asking myself some questions helped me figure out where I was on my spiritual journey.

In the Old Testament, God called men and women to his purpose through direct means. He interrupted their lives. But after the Holy Spirit came, this wasn't necessary.

There are only a few instances in the New Testament when God dramatically called someone to their more. We will look at the two of them later. But now we have God's word and the Holy Spirit to lead us, which is how most Christians find their more.

Reflection

This book encourages you to consider the idea of more. It benefits all Christians to take some time periodically to reflect on their lives. We can become static in our faith, just like in our lives. The status quo can be pretty comfortable, so it's good to take some time for reflection.

I often remind myself that I've been sitting too long if my spot on the sofa is identifiable by my butt print. Well, the same is true with our spiritual lives. We are designed for movement, and that means spiritual movement as well.

The Bible encourages reflection in several places:

- Haggai 1:5-7 (consider our ways)
- Lamentations 3:40 (examine our ways)
- Psalm 139:23-24,2 Corinthians 13:3-5 (test ourselves)
- Galatians 6:4 (examine our work)
- Psalms 139: 23-24 (Search me, O, God.)

The Bible has a lot to say about healthy self-examination. Self-examination is how we evaluate our walk with God.

Men and women who are serious about their faith have engaged in self-reflection throughout the centuries. Jesus took significant amounts of time for reflection. Many Christians visit monasteries for a few days of deep thinking. I don't think I could do that, but I'd like to try just once. However, I do set aside time to sit, think, and reflect every year.

The will of God

In one sense, if we genuinely seek God's will and walk closely with him, we fulfill our part in his overall plan. God is God and works out all things, including your life, according to his purposes. But God has a specific call, a more, for each of us. It's hard for some Christians to believe this. Maybe I should say they don't want to believe it, for if they believe it, they are accountable for fulfilling it.

But first, let me tell you a story. I use a little phrase with God when he surprises me, which he often does. I will look up, laugh, and ask, "God, how did you do that?"

I had been spending a lot of time thinking about this book. Writing this book is more challenging than my first one because I'm in new territory. I knew God had specific plans for people, but I wasn't sure how to present the information clearly. I wanted to explain the concept in a way that would excite and motivate people.

I mean, haven't we all sat through sermons that presented many good truths but missed them because the words were "heavy"? (Am I the only one? Please tell me I'm not.)

One. We all know, for example, that the concepts in God's word apply to all of us. The first and greatest commandment, to love God and treat our neighbors how we want to be treated, is a commandment for us irrespective of our more. It is God's will for _all_ Christians. When we follow this commandment, we follow God's will, his revealed will, for all Christians. That's where we all begin.

___Two.___ Can God accomplish his plans regardless of whether a person picks up their specific personal more? Of course. But God has reasons for asking each of us to do what he asks. He wants our unique stamp on it. And he wants us to experience the blessing that comes from our obedience to our more.

The Potter alone knows why he formed a piece of clay as he did. But there is always a specific reason. Back to the story.

I was still in the thinking stages of this book, especially about the specific mores. We were at our cabin, and I took a day to visit the local mission store, where I usually find books for free. Seriously. For a book nut like me, that's better than frosting on a bakery birthday cake, and I love bakery frosting on a bakery cake!

I was looking through the books and found one called *When Faith and Decisions Collide*. It sounded interesting, so I took it. Free, remember? (By the way, I donate more than I take. It's like my personal lending library.)

I couldn't tell what the book was about by the title. When I got to the cabin and looked at the chapter outline, you know what it was, don't you? It was all about God's will.

"How do you do that, God? Every time?"

(I could fill a book with many stories like this. Hmm.) God provides me with resources for every question I come up with, even those I haven't asked.

Come to think of it, maybe I should ask more questions.

After I read the book, I had a more precise understanding of the will of God. I will refer to God's will as his revealed will to all believers and his specific will as it applies to each unique follower. But this is just for discussion purposes. It's all his will.

___Three.___ God's revealed will applies to every believer, and everything we need to accomplish God's will is in his word. I Peter 1:3, "By his divine power, God has given us everything we need for living a godly life. We have received all of this by coming to know Him."

For some groups of believers and denominations, though, it stops here. They believe, for example, that if you follow God's revealed will, whatever choices you make in life are already sanctioned by God. It doesn't matter what profession you choose or whom you marry because you are in his will, etc.

God's overall will *does* guide our choices. Don't most Christians believe that?

God has a specific plan for my life, your life, and specific mores that only we can accomplish. The Bible is full of such examples. God's specific more might be explained as a deeper personal level of God's revealed will. And there's too much evidence in God's word not to believe that God has a specific plan for each of us.

Does anyone believe that someone other than the Apostle Paul could have written or done what he did? No. Do you believe Christ would have appeared to just anyone on that road to Emmaus?

My example. No one but me could have written my book about depression from my point of view or my experience. Someone other than me could have certainly written a book about depression, and of course, many have, but only I could write this book from my viewpoint. Someone needs to read my words because they appeal to them more than other authors, just like particular authors, and their words appeal more to me.

Can we walk outside God's will? Of course. God allows us to make mistakes. He does all he can to help us avoid them, but we are stubborn people, some more so than others. (Me, pointing my thumb at myself.) We want our own way. Many Christians have a skewed idea that God sends everyone to a mission field far away if they dare seek his specific will for their lives. While this book isn't about God's will, you need to understand the premise under which I write. Our more, our purpose is found in his specific, deeper will for us, and that doesn't necessarily mean a far-off mission field.

As we obey God's revealed will, he directs us more specifically. Some areas include who we marry, our vocation, and other crucial decisions. Is there only one person we should marry? Only one vocation we should choose?

God's specific will is that he provides a limited field of choices, but within that limited field, there are still choices. As we mature in our faith, we walk a narrow path but one that, at the same time, is still wide with possibilities. God mentions wide places in several places in the Bible.

I love what Tony Evans writes in his commentary, *The Tony*

Evans Bible Commentary.

"As followers of Jesus, believers have been placed on earth to carry out God's will according to their spiritual gifts and his plan for each life. Your calling is unique to you. Its fulfillment often involves an intersection of your past experiences, passions, gifts, skills, position, and personality. (Acts 13:36; Galatians 2:20; Ephesians 2:10; Philippians 2:12-13.)

It's like being in an airport and waiting for your flight. God has invited everyone Christian to the airport, and he's got a flight destination for each of us. When we decide we are committed to the call of God on our lives, God will intervene, interject, and do whatever he needs to do to get us to the right destination.

Knowing God's purpose, or more, for our lives, is never restricting. The possibilities are abundant.

So, let's not be confused. God's will, as revealed in his word, is straightforward. We walk in faith while God opens and shuts doors, and as he does, we come closer to knowing his particular plan for us. The more we know his revealed will, the more we discern the special call or purpose God created for us.

At some point, God's will becomes more specific, and we find that unique plan just for us. Once we identify it, there are still choices to make because God is not a puppet master deciding everything for us.

Let me use my growth journey as an example. As a new follower of Christ, I couldn't narrow my focus, as is true with any new believer. There was so much to learn, so much to know. I tried on a lot of "hats."

But if you seek a closer walk with God and remain true to his word, you *will* find your more, your purpose. You don't have to fret about it, but it deserves thought.

Yes, we can live our Christian life without considering God's unique plan for us, and our standing in Christ remains firm. We are just as forgiven, just as loved, and still heaven-bound. There is no question about any of that.

But to find that unique purpose or mission is the more. And who doesn't want more?

In this book, I will examine categories of the mores as I see them. I will distinguish between mores that were permanent and those that weren't. For example, Judas's wrong mores were permanent, but Lot's weren't. Some mores, such as Ruth's, highlight a specific period in the person's life. Some examples could fit into multiple categories.

I Kings 11 states that God was angry with Solomon. God warned him twice about having nothing to do with foreign gods. But Solomon didn't listen. His story could have fit into a couple of categories.

Some examples are from a short snapshot of a person's life. There were many examples to use and many ways to categorize them. Finally, though, I had to decide. I also found that having the same number of stories for each category wasn't necessary. Once I made my point, I stopped.

Finally

We begin our search for that answer by looking at examples in the scriptures of those who pursued wrong mores.

In the book's first half, I will give examples of men and women in the Bible who pursued their more within the categories I listed earlier. Remember, I could have placed some of them in more than one category but chose to pick what I felt was the most obvious. The second half of the book will list helpful tools for finding your more and can be downloaded from my website, goodthoughtsgoodlives.com

I hope you enjoy this journey.

FOUR: THE CATEGORIES

Wrong mores:

- Lot
- Jonah
- Haman
- Judas

Right mores:

- Noah
- Joseph
- Ruth
- Daniel

Detoured mores:

- Israelites
- Jacob
- Rahab
- Peter

Thrust-upon mores:

- Esther
- Job
- Mary, mother of Jesus
- Paul

Back-burner mores:

- Moses
- Joshua
- John Mark

Thrown-Away mores:

- Adam and Eve
- Esau
- Solomon
- Ananias and Saphira
- Rich Young Ruler.

Desperate mores:

- Mary Magdalene
- Woman bent over
- The man whose son was dying

Little known mores:

- Ehud
- Jethro
- Jael
- Jabez
- Anne Frank

Unworthy mores:

- Alice Walker

Quiet mores:

- Various examples

But it's important to know that all of these categories have moving parts. For example, a right more can become a wrong more and vice versa. A delayed more can get back on the right track. A lost more can be found. God is a God of second chances. If you decide, for example, that you've thrown away your more, God can help you find it or reframe a new one. If it's detoured or delayed, depending on who is doing the detouring or delaying, you can get back on track. God *can* do anything. He *will* do anything to see his purpose carried out.

FIVE: ASPECTS OF MORE

This book's theme encourages you to look deeper at your life, dreams, talents, abilities, strengths, weaknesses, and all you are in Christ. It enables you to evaluate how you are fulfilling God's unique plan.

The title of the devotional that I and thousands of others read daily is *My Utmost for His Highest*, by Oswald Chambers. Don't we all want to know we are giving our utmost for His highest?

Finding our more is about moving within God's revealed will, walking through our typical days, being open to the possibilities, and believing that God will lead us to our more.

God reveals our more when we understand it and are ready to receive it. One of my all-time favorite sayings isn't even from scripture, but I'll bet I could find verification for it in the Bible if I looked hard enough. Its authorship is unknown.

"When the student is ready, the teacher will appear."

As Christians, we know this is true. We need only look to Jesus and the disciples. Would anyone disagree that Jesus showed up when the disciples were ready? Jesus could have shown up earlier, or he could have waited a few years. But he showed up at precisely the right time. The students were ready, whether or not they knew it. But even at that, the disciples had a long way to go. There was a lot to learn. And just because Jesus showed up didn't mean they were all on board immediately. It's the same with us.

When I first discovered my own more, I balked. Oh, not because I felt directed to write *a* book, but a specific book. A book about my struggles with depression, how I overcame it, and how what I learned could help others. It revealed way too much about me. I wasn't ready for the criticism. But I wrote anyway, knowing it was my more and trusting God would make it succeed.

I wished it had been as dramatic as the burning bush, God's booming voice, or even like the gentle wind that spoke to Elijah, but it wasn't. Each step I took led to another, like a progressive revelation. It got to where when I picked up any book, read anything online, or listened to a podcast, I found even more affirmation. I was drawn to something bigger than myself.

Finding our more is like that for most of us. Very few of us will wake up one day and say, "Yeah, I've found it! I've found my more!" It will likely come after many jumps and starts, as well as successes and failures. It will be more like unearthing many layers. Eventually, everything will point in that direction and fall into place. A sense of unexplainable peace settles over you, and you know. It will be like the peace in Philippians 4:7, "a peace that passes understanding."

When I am writing, I think of nothing else. It's hard because I want to make this message clear yet effortless. I want to be faithful to God's word. Most importantly, I have no doubts I am fulfilling my more. While I might get frustrated, I never lose my sense of mission. I find my greatest joy in sitting at this computer and writing.

The realization

That's it. Even as I write, I know that's what I've been waltzing around.

When you find your more, you will have no doubts. It won't matter what anyone else thinks. It won't matter how hard it is. It won't count the hours you have to work. None of it will matter because you will experience such passion and wholeness that you will feel like a new person. You will have a reason to get up in the morning and fall asleep peacefully at night. Life will be more rewarding.

The purpose of writing this book is to encourage anyone who reads it to look for the more God has for them. Some of you will discover you are already there, but now it's confirmed. You will have reflected and concluded that you are following your more. For some, my words will find a responsive chord in you because you have been wondering about this yourself. Perhaps now will be the time to think it through. You're reading this book, so that's half the journey already.

My husband and I were on our daily walk, and I ran my thinking by him. I asked him if he'd ever thought about his purpose in life. His answer was simple. "My purpose is to love God, care for my family, and do it all the best I know." That's his purpose. He is content with that. And, I should add, he does a great job in all those areas.

My husband is one of those rare individuals whose purpose and passions, his more, have always been clear to him. He's always known his more. He pursues it even though the specifics have changed and evolved. However, he doesn't remain stagnant because he already knows his purpose. He started where we should all start, with the greatest commandment, which I will discuss later. He gets that right, and the rest unfolds for him as he lives his daily life.

I'm passionate about home decorating, DIY-ing, and many creative pursuits. But they aren't my more, my purpose. I've tried to use them within the context of being a Christ-follower, but I've always known they were only hobbies. As a young woman, I knew I had the gift of teaching and encouragement, and I have used them in various ways since I became a follower of Christ at sixteen. (I admit, sadly, though, there were years when my gifts were ill-represented.) But I came to a place where I felt the uneasiness that comes when we know something else is beckoning us. It's like a slippery piece of Jell-O that keeps slipping through our fingers.

My husband is already living his more. But what about those who struggle to define their purpose and passion, their more, as his wife did? (I will use the words passion, purpose, and more interchangeably from now on.)

The asking

The minute we ask ourselves if there could be another dimension to our gifts, we are on our way. When we wonder if God has called us *to do something more on our faith journey, it's precisely because he has.* The questioning in our mind is the whisper of the Holy Spirit; otherwise, those thoughts would not be there.

But sad to say, many people never get there. Why is that do you suppose? My thought is that the word "more" itself sounds somewhat self-indulgent. More. Really? Aren't we Christians supposed to settle for what we've got? Aren't we supposed to be grateful and not ask for more? Isn't it somewhat self-centered to think we should have more? Isn't that how some people in the Bible found themselves in a lot of trouble? Wanting more? Like Haman. (Wait till you read his story.)

The book of Esther is one of my favorite books of the Bible, but not for the reasons you might think. While Esther is an example of obedience and bravery, we learn even more from Haman and how his quest for the wrong more cost him his life. He's one of my favorite villains. That sounds like an oxymoron if I've ever heard of one. A favorite villain? But he reminds me so much of the issues that bring disaster into our lives. He's such a perfect example of someone who wanted more, all right, but not the right more. But all that is for the next chapter.

More is the deep longing in our hearts that shouts we are lacking something, that we feel the need for something more—like the perfect latte. Most lattes taste good, but what makes them taste great? For me, it's usually an extra shot of foam. Or it's the meal we're enjoying well enough but lacking that unique blend of seasonings to be delicious. Or, for me, it's the dessert. Our more is like a fantastic latte, a delicious meal, or a special dessert that makes our mouths water. When we eat it, we are thoroughly satiated.

We might already be using our spiritual gifts, but God is asking us to take them further. God might call us to refine or polish our more. Our mores continue to change and evolve as God opens up new opportunities and as we grow in our spiritual walk.

To repeat:

Our more is progressive and ever-changing but always remains under the umbrella of our spiritual gifts.

The fear

My more for this period in my life is writing. I am called to write. Deep down inside, I knew I should write to publish, but frankly, I was frightened to pursue it. I still am.

My first book is published for all to read and criticize. (I haven't received any yet, however. Whew!) But the fear surfaced again with this book. And that fear of criticism stops many of us. I would suggest that the fear of criticism holds most of us back. What will people think? Here's an example that will make you chuckle.

I've had my first book signing as I write this book. Do you know what my biggest fear that night was? That someone would say something negative about my book. Duh! It was a book signing. They were buying books, and I was signing them. Think about that for a minute. They hadn't even read them yet! So that was fear wasted, as most fears are. You may find your more, but it might scare you.

Before I ever typed words into my computer, I was "writing" in a different form, conducting workshops and retreats. I lead

Bible studies. I spoke for various organizations, guided retreats, and worked as a hospital chaplain. But I didn't see those avenues as writing, yet every one of those tasks required writing first. That's what I mean by progressive.

Each ministry took me one step closer to becoming an author. I didn't know it, but God did. Proverbs 3:5- 6 is one of one hundred verses I memorized in a contest when I was about sixteen. (I'm competitive.) I love that I can look back and see the truth of those verses.

My more for this period in my life is writing. I am called to write. Deep down inside, I knew I should write to publish, but frankly, I was frightened to pursue it. I still am.

The joy

The New Testament church grew, and people were excited about their faith.

Though traumatic, the New Testament account of the church's beginnings was exciting. People were sharing their possessions (although two we will learn about later weren't and met a disastrous outcome) and getting together in their homes for meals and worship. You don't do that if you're miserable. That early church was on fire with their more.

However, as the church grew, the uneducated learned to read, others with different opinions joined, and churches felt the need to organize. The apostle Paul addressed church organization often. The church became an institution in addition to being a church; therefore, it needed a hierarchy and organizational charts.

Consequently, the New Testament church started doing what the Pharisees and Sadducees did years earlier. They became overly religious and concerned more with rules than righteousness, the very thing Jesus condemned! Someone must have come up with the numbskull idea of, "Hey, should we be enjoying this?". Soon, the church started looking different, instituting rules and regulations that killed the joy.

In his epistles, the apostle Paul often addressed this lack of joy, urging everyone to put Christ first and love each other. History shows they returned to their old ways once Paul wasn't around to keep them on track. We are still there today, with many churches being an institution first and a church second. Christians should be discerning about the leadership of their churches, including their pastors. Churches can quickly fall away from the truth when the gospel is not central in the pulpit.

Any time faith is too narrowly and rigidly defined, anytime man piles on unnecessary regulations and hierarchy, joy flies right out the window. Not to mention our more.

The question for churches is, "Why do we settle for less when the Bible is all about the more?" I hope to answer that.

When you find your more, it will bring you joy. How do I know that? Because anytime we are in the center of God's will, we experience joy. We are in God's will when we embrace our more. So, you could conclude that if you are genuinely joyful and content in your faith and know you are doing what God has called you to, you have already found your more.

Two things can be true at the same time. We can be truly joyful, but there might yet be another level God has called us to and even more joy. It never hurts to examine our faith periodically so it doesn't remain stagnant.

And if you are still reading this book, it means you think this might also be true for you. And maybe some greater joy. If there is even the tiniest question, it suggests God is asking you to open yourself up to the possibility of more in your life.

The roadblock

Do you know the most significant roadblock most people face with their more? It isn't fear, although fear is certainly a roadblock. It isn't doubt, although there is usually some. The biggest roadblock is the hard work that might be required. I wasn't too worried when I knew my purpose was to write a book. I have the gift of gab, and I enjoy writing so easy-peasy. Right?

No. Oh, so wrong.

It wasn't the idea of hard work that hindered me because I am not afraid of hard work. But the hard work, other than the writing, almost made me give up. Had I known the hours I would spend on everything *but* the writing, like reading, researching, Bible study, and the countless other mundane tasks required to write a book, I might have turned a deaf ear. (Like today, when my editing program indicates I have over a thousand corrections to make! Primarily because of how I use the word "more." The app doesn't like it all.)

Some of my best thoughts and ideas came when I couldn't write them down, like driving or waking up in the middle of the night. So, I had to figure out how to capture them. That involved learning how to use the memo function on my phone. Having a notebook by the bed in case I wake up in the middle of the night with some profound thoughts. And a notebook in the car when waiting at a red light.

Or the times I would cloister myself at my desk and write till my fingers grew tired, my eyes looked like I hadn't slept in a week, and my back was sore. But maybe the worst part was when I thought I wasn't any good. (Yes, even though I know my more, I still question.) I would be less than honest if I didn't say I thought God might have had it wrong this time.

Yep, that's all part of the more. But guess what? All the frustrations above have been nothing compared to the joy and peace I experienced this past year. I feel more alive, creative, and on fire for God than ever. I find myself in a wonderful, free place where I feel no need to explain myself to anyone. That's what finding my purpose has done for me. I believe knowing your purpose will do that for you as well.

If we were all using our God-given gifts and abilities to their fullest, heaven's ears would explode from all the shouts of praise here on earth. The angels and those Heaven-dwellers that have preceded us would dance in joy and celebration. People would see our joy and passion, and our pleasing fragrance would draw them to Christ. Ultimately, this is what our more is all about:

showing the way to Christ.

But what if your more turns out to be one of the "flashy" ones, meaning yours will be public? First of all, it doesn't make you special. On the contrary, it makes you very accountable. Trust me, I know.

Writers aren't more special because they write. Artists aren't more special because they paint. Pastors aren't more special because they preach, or worship leaders more special because they lead. A young mom lovingly caring for her children, a grandfather maintaining an active relationship with his grandchildren, a server who goes beyond what she needs, each has a more that is just as special.

No one's more, no purpose or mission, is more significant than any other. One more gets no more applause from heaven than another. It's an equal-opportunity kind of thing. The reward is knowing we've been faithful to *our* calling. Yet many people compare their calling to others, and that's a mistake.

Mores change over the years, but did you know they can also shrink? But that's not a bad thing. A shrinking more is still a more, but it might not require as much as it once did or be smaller in scope. The responsibility may have shifted. It could be that we physically cannot continue our more within its current parameters. A shrinking more might mean your more is over in its present form, but another might be around the corner. I think I can explain a shrinking more like this.

I have had several foot surgeries. I love to hike. I still do it, but now I rethink it because of those physical limitations. I use a walking stick if I'm hiking now because my feet don't always feel the ground beneath them as they should. But do I still love hiking? Absolutely. I just do it differently.

As we age, our more might shrink because of ill health or simply less energy or mobility. But that doesn't mean we still don't have the same more. Someone with the gift of teaching might find another way to express it. A shrinking more doesn't mean a "less" more; it just means a smaller scale more. For example, someone can use their teaching gift in numerous ways as they age.

There was a time when I did a lot of public speaking. Now, I write instead of travel. Is that a shrinking more? Geographically, it is. But in every other way, it's bigger.

Shrinking mores, however, is not a category I included in this book, which is why I provided the above discussion.

The accountability

There is a flip side as well. Our more brings additional responsibility with it as well. "To whom much is given, much is required." Luke 12:48. We are accountable for how we use our more. When we think of accountability, we find the best example in the parable in Matthew 25:14-30.

A master gave each of his three servants varying amounts of money. To one, he gave five talents. One servant received two, and to one, he gave one talent. The two who received the five and two talents each doubled the amount. The one given the least amount hid it away. Isn't that like a lot of us? We hide our gifts and talents because we don't think they're big enough to work with in the first place. Why do we do that, do you suppose? I believe there are four reasons why.

1. We don't think it's significant enough. We see our gift as so small we might as well keep it to ourselves. So, instead of taking a leap of faith and seeing where it goes, we bury it.
2. We don't want to do the work to develop it.
3. We fear where it might take us. We fear the judgment of others. "What will people think?" I knew I could write a book but feared judgment (like the worker who buried his money). Even though I had good reasons, I dug a hole and buried it for some years. But while I waited to dig it up, I began blogging as a substitute. As it turned out, blogging was the backdoor I used to write about the subjects my published works eventually centered around.
4. We don't want to work. If you want to know what the Bible says about laziness, read the book of Proverbs. I read a chapter a day and have for years. I am always surprised by how often the Proverbs address laziness. I guess God knew it would be a problem for many of us. Back to our parable.

The manager was very pleased with the two servants who increased their gift. These two servants each invested differently, but both increased their original investment two-fold. Neither of the two received commendation because of the increase in amount, but only because they wisely used the talents given to them. The increased amount was unimportant; only what was done with it. A little ability, talent, and hard work can accomplish miracles.

But then there is the third servant. He took his money, the same amount as the other two, dug a hole, and buried it. His master was most displeased with him and soundly reamed him out.

Because this is a parable, there is a lesson for us to learn.

We can dig a spiritual hole and hide our talents, or we can multiply them many times over. God gave all of us talents we can share with the world. He will reward us depending on how faithful we are in using them.

In my first book, I share a scene that I play out in my head, especially when I'm writing.

I'm at Heaven's Gate. Jesus is holding a box, a box set aside for me the day I was only a thought in God's mind. In that box were all the talents and abilities assigned to me by the Great Assigner. As I walk toward Jesus, I know he will open the box. How my heart will sing when Jesus sees the box is empty. Blogging and writing are me emptying my box.

We all have a "box" full of gifts to share. Don't you want to empty yours?

The timing

Certainly, when we're busy with a growing family or beginning a career, our more is about as more as it can get. Of course, some people do manage to do both, but, in my opinion, they are rare. But some people have about as much more as they can handle. They might prefer some less.

In those cases, their more can develop over time through the sharpening of their skills and talents. When the time is right, they can move out in faith, putting their personal and unique more into action. God knows our circumstances, and his timing is always right. We won't miss it as long as we are following our shepherd. He will always lead us on the right path.

What if you're one of those who know your more but have had to put it on hold? Now, you fear you've missed your opportunity. Briefly said, you haven't. If that dream has stayed alive in you, it can only mean you are to investigate all the possibilities that present themselves now. God will redeem your time. He certainly did mine.

Can we achieve the same level of success if we start late? I guess that all depends. And mostly, that depends on God. Do we miss moments when there was the right time to do something? I don't know. I can't answer that because God's timing is elusive and mysterious. But what I know to be true is this: God has a special mission for each of us, and he *will* reveal it. If we diligently seek God, he will show us our more and use us despite missed opportunities. Do you honestly believe God would do otherwise?

I was older when I started writing and full of doubt. While I knew there were valid reasons I hadn't pursued publishing earlier, I still worried I had waited too long. Age is one of those parameters in our lives that always seem somewhat slippery. We feel too young, or we feel too old. When I was only sixteen, my pastor asked me to share my faith story with other churches. I wonder how many people scoffed at me because of my age. But I had already lived through more than most of them.

We tangle up many of our dreams with the limitations we think age places on us. Read about men and women in scripture who were at opposite ends of the age spectrum, from David to Moses. Most of them used age as an excuse in the beginning as well. But it never worked. God kept pursuing them. Besides, who knows when the right time is for anything? Oh, I know the answer to that, God.

If we feel too old to seek our more, it means we think life has already passed us by. Frankly, I hope I never feel that way. I hope there is never a day I can't find some more that God has for me. That's what makes life exciting. But then others feel too young and immature. Who's going to listen to them? Who knows that right now might be your "for such-a-time-as-this" moment?

But most of you who read this book have another issue preventing you from seeking more. You probably don't feel worthy enough in God's kingdom even to warrant one. You feel untalented, ungifted, or insignificant. Oh, you believe there are mores, just not for you. Well, join the crowd of almost everybody who has accomplished anything.

We all look around and compare ourselves to others and come

up short. It's just human nature. There is only one time when comparing ourselves to others is a good idea: if it motivates us to accomplish something good.

Comparisons lead to discouragement. The other thing comparisons do is give us an excuse because as long we can play the poor-me-I'm-just-not-that-special card, we are off the hook. So, we think anyway.

There isn't a single excuse in scripture where God has said, *"Oh, well, if you don't feel like it, I understand. You don't have to do it. You're excused."* I know some of you are thinking about how God allowed Aaron to speak for Moses because Moses claimed his speaking skills were insufficient for the task. But Moses quickly started speaking for himself. No one knows why God gave him an out initially, but that's God's business, not ours. Excuses don't work with God. Go back and read the earlier parable about the servants.

The question we all ask

Shortly before my mother died, she asked: "What was I put on earth for?" She constantly compared herself to others and came up short. She never thought she had any talent, and now she couldn't even practice the only more she knew. For her, that more meant taking care of her family, and her abilities were in a cruel prison of dementia. I would love to say I spoke beautiful words of encouragement to her, that I lifted her spirits, and that she felt much better by my profound words of wisdom.

All I could say was, "Mom, you are on this earth for me. I don't know what I'll do without you." Not very profound, and I wish I had said so much more. But it was all I could say. I think that was because I've asked myself that question and haven't always had the answer, either. It's the existential question that everyone asks themselves at least once. What am I on earth for? Why was I created?

SIX: WRONG MORES

Where do we begin? What constitutes a wrong more?

Remember, right mores are God-directed and God-honoring and are outward-directed, so the definition of a wrong more has to be the opposite. And it is. Wrong mores are *not* God-directed, *nor* are they God-honoring. They are self-seeking, selfish, glory-seeking, self-indulgent, etc. It is never for the benefit of anyone other than us. They are never God's will for us, and God will never anoint them.

We have less joy, less fulfillment, and less of everything. We might try to convince ourselves for a time that it is all good, and maybe it is. Still, when it's in the middle of the night, and we wake up in a panic because we might lose it all, we know at an intuitive level that we wrongly gained our more.

We can have a more that isn't from God. And the interesting part about that is that a more that isn't from God always ends up being *less*. Wrong mores can make us miserable, but not always. We all know people who take the wrong paths and yet seem happy. Maybe. But as the Bible states in Proverbs 23:7, "As a man thinks in his heart, so he is." Anyone can deceive themself.

So, where do we begin? Well, we could start with the obvious: Adam and Eve. They had it all, and yet they wanted more. The same with Jacob and Esau. Esau had it all, too, but he gave it away because he didn't value it. We'll discuss these two examples later in another category. For now, we start with Lot.

Lot

First, I have an admission. I have a problem with how Lot is spoken of as a man of faith in 2 Peter 2: 7-8. In the story I will share, he certainly isn't a man of faith. But we must remember that the incident we will look at is just one small snapshot of his life. If someone took a snapshot of our lives when we acted less than noble, would we look any better? So, I'll give him a pass. Besides, if the Bible states Lot was a man of faith, I assume he learned his lessons and proved his faith over his remaining years.

Lot's story begins with his uncle, Abram. Terah, Abram's father, felt led by God to move the entire family to the Ur of the Chaldees and eventually the land of Canaan. They stopped in Haran, where they remained until Terah died at 205 years of age. We don't know why Terah moved, but God does. We only know he proceeded to go to Canaan but never got there.

Terah was rich, and most scholars assume he was a pagan who worshipped foreign gods. The city of Haran was the center of such idol worship, which might explain why he moved no further. Maybe he just got comfortable, and the thought of moving again was too much. But while in Haran, his youngest son, Lot's father, died, and his uncle Abram more or less adopted his nephew, Lot.

After the family patriarch, Terah, also dies, God speaks to Abram and tells him to continue to Canaan, where he will become the father of many nations. Many scholars have wondered why Abram was told to move. The Koran and Jewish tradition suggest that Abram refused to worship the local gods and that King Nimrod of Ur found out. A prophet told the king that a man would rise against him, and the king worried that man might be Abram. Abram feared for his life and the lives of his family, so he left Ur.

Abram is seventy-five when God encounters him, and this is God's first personal encounter with someone outside of the Garden of Eden. This encounter was foreign to Abraham. Hearing God personally was probably why he obeyed so readily. Talk about a more coming later in life. Although people lived longer back then, Abram was no spring chicken. But God didn't see Abram's age as an issue.

Now is an excellent place to stop and see how God views time. You and I think of days, weeks, months, years. God has no such reference. He thinks of time in terms of eternity. But we place parameters around ourselves and believe we are too young or old to pursue more. God isn't looking at you within those constraints. We don't have to comprehend time as God does. If you sense a more for you, throw out any sense of age restrictions. God will work around those. 2 Peter 3:8 "...one day is as a thousand years with the LORD and a thousand years as one day."

Abram and his immediate extended family dwelt in Canaan until famine. Because of the ensuing starvation, they moved farther south to Egypt, where they settled. Abram acquires vast wealth and livestock and inherits his father's inheritance.

Because of the sizeable numbers of livestock each family owned and only so much pasture, the two groups of herdsmen argued. Abram didn't like this fuss, so he amicably suggested to Lot that they divide the land. Abram was generous with his suggestion and gave Lot his choice of land to the north or the south. By default, Abram would take the leftover land. In other words, Lot got first dibs.

But Lot wanted the portion of land he'd had his eyes on, the Jordan Valley, which was lush and well-irrigated. To Lot, the Jordan Valley was "like the garden of the LORD." Abram gave him the requested land without hesitation, and Abram moved south. Lot wanted the greener pastures but soon learned that greener isn't necessarily better. Lot chose his more because it looked better.

In case you don't know what happened next, Lot pitched his tent close to Sodom. He might have wanted to be near the hustle and bustle of a bigger city. When describing evil, we often refer to Sodom and Gomorrah because corruption was so prevalent in those two cities. There is no evidence that Lot was a part of this.

God decides to destroy the two cities because of all the evil. But before that, a battle ensues, and rival countries attack Sodom and Gomorrah. The rival nations win and take Lot and his family captive. Abram learns of this, and in Genesis 14:16, we read how he rescues Lot.

Sometime after this, three "men" (two angels and the Lord himself) come to visit Abram. Abram learns of God's impending plan to destroy Sodom and Gomorrah. Because Lot is living there (apparently after Abram rescued him, he returned to live in Sodom), Abram begins "bargaining" with God. Ultimately, God spares Lot, his wife, and his two daughters-in-law from the initial destruction of the cities. However, Lot's wife dies as they are running from the enemy. That's another exciting story.

Lot wanted much "more" than he was entitled to. Think about it. Abram didn't have to take Lot to Haran in the first place. Lot should have insisted that Abram have first dibs. Lot's greediness, his "more," almost killed his entire family. While we can be critical of Lot, we must remember that we, too, have been in a position like Lot. When given a choice, we have taken the best even though we haven't deserved it.

Sometimes, our more may not look like it in the beginning. Abram took the less desirable land and became the father of multiple nations. That's a "more" if I've ever heard of one.

Do we have to ask whose choice was the best? Remember, your "more" might look like "less" initially. Don't judge your more as less important because it's less "flashy." A more is a more is a more.

Jesus tackled this argument when an argument ensued in Luke 9:46: "An argument started among them, (the disciples) as to who might be the greatest." Jesus quickly diffused this argument.

Abraham took the less desirable land and became the father of multiple nations. That's a more if I've ever heard of one. Lot is never mentioned again except in 2 Peter 7 & 8, where it reads that Lot was tormented "over their lawless deeds that he saw and heard."

Lot's story: Genesis 11:27-32 and Genesis, chapters 12-14.

Jonah

Jonah, Jonah, Jonah.

Jonah was a prophet. His job was to preach, and God told him to preach to the Ninevites. So, where's the problem? Well, Jonah didn't like this particular more, even though it came from God himself.

Many people think Jonah is an allegory. But 2 Kings 14:25 refers to Jonah as an accredited prophet from Gath-Hepher near Nazareth. Also, Jesus treats Jonah's story as factual in Matthew: 12-39-41. So that settles it for me.

In verse one, Jonah hears his call. God makes it clear what his more is and gives him detailed instructions. He is to preach to Ninevah about their wickedness, with the goal being their redemption.

But right away, in verse two, Jonah takes a ship to head as far away from Ninevah as possible, Tarshish. He didn't even take the time to process it. He skedaddles and finds a ship to get as far away from God as possible. Why? Because he didn't like this race of people. He had good reason, though.

The Ninevites were known to engage in idolatrous worship

and extreme cruelty to prisoners of war. But in any ethnic population, there are good people. Jonah did what we do: he lumped a whole group of people together and hated them for what only some of them did.

(I find that interesting. I mean, Jonah was a prophet. He had a history with God. So, why did he think he could run away? But then, why do we? Be careful that as you discover your purpose, your more, that you don't run away just because you don't like it.)

A massive storm blows up, and waves batter the ship. The men on board have learned of Jonah's disobedience and blame him for the weather. And it's interesting to note that it takes a pagan to tell a prophet to pray. At least this time, Jonah does the right thing and tells the men to throw him overboard so God's punishment won't land on them.

They do.

An enormous fish swallows Jonah, and he sits in that smelly gunk for three days. And, of course, he prays. Wouldn't we all if we were stuck in the belly of something that unpleasant? Suddenly, Jonah likes God again.

God graciously hears his prayers and makes the whale vomit him out. Once again, God reiterates Jonah's more. "Go to Ninevah." Jonah does what he is supposed to do this time, although begrudgingly. And when the Ninevites *do* repent, which God wanted, Jonah is resentful because he wanted fire and brimstone to be showered on them. He has been preaching their destruction for years, *per God's instructions,* and now they repent?

He feels foolish, as if he wasted his time preaching against them. He feels blind-sighted by God himself. But instead of admitting it, he tells God, "God, that's why I ran to Tarshish. I knew you would relent and save the Ninevites. So why did I end up with egg all over my face? Just take my life, LORD." In other words, "Why didn't you do all this in the first place? I knew you would anyway, and it would've saved me a lot of embarrassment."

Jonah knew God to be a loving and merciful God. And as long as that love and mercy were showered on Jonah and *his* people, it was great. But Jonah didn't like it when he thought God might spare his nation's enemy.

Jonah was God's prophet to Israel, not to Ninevah. His patriotism and love for his nation made him question God's command. He was ready to incur God's displeasure, abandon his profession, and risk the safety of his own country.

Jonah never wanted his more. Or at least the parts he didn't like. He only wanted God's presence when it went along with Jonah's own plans. The story of Jonah ends on a grim note. He gets mad. God asks Jonah what right he has to be angry. Jonah doesn't answer but goes off by himself in a huff and sulks under a handmade shelter. But it gets scorching hot, and the shelter isn't enough, so God mercifully supplies a vine (obviously more of a bush or tree) to shade him from the sun.

The next day, Jonah still hasn't quit sulking, and God has had it this time. He supplies a worm to eat down the plant, removing

Jonah's shelter, and on top of that, God sends a hot wind, making Jonah even more miserable. The last we see of Jonah is when he is sulking under the scorching sun, fuming with anger. What a way to be remembered.

Most Christians see the story of Jonah as centered on being swallowed by a whale and then rescued after three days. It represents the death and resurrection of Jesus. And that it is all true. But I think the story of Jonah is also about Jonah's "more." It wasn't just a whale that swallowed him. Personal shallowness swallowed Jonah.

As you recall, Jonah knew his mission from the very beginning. He didn't have to search it out. It was there right along. For some of you reading this, you know your more, too. But, like Jonah, you don't want to pursue it.

I get it. More can be scary. Mine was. But it shouldn't make us miserable. If it does, we have somehow misinterpreted it. Like Jonah, we've allowed our feelings to get in the way. God never intended for Jonah to be so unhappy and angry. I wonder if God ever regretted giving Jonah his more. I sure would have.

There is something else we shouldn't overlook, which might be hard to admit. Have you ever read a story about a repentant person who never really suffers the consequences of their pre-Christian ways, and you think, "That's just not right?" Or a family member becomes a Christian, and they act all holy now, and you resent it.

If you tell me you never think these same things, I want to meet you because I've never met a saint. We've all been like Jonah at some point in our lives. It's not fun to admit, but if we don't, we'll have a temper tantrum and sit in the scorching sun with no shade.

There have been days when I've been writing, and it has been a miserable experience. My computer hiccups: my thoughts wander everywhere, and I get distracted. But that's all about me. I'm the one that has allowed myself to feel that way. When I step away and return the next day, my more is exciting once again.

If Jonah had just stepped away instead of running away, his story might have ended on a high note.

Can you trust that the journey doesn't have to be miserable no matter where it takes you? I don't believe God ever asks us to do something we hate.

In a way, Jonah was a racist. What, you think racism didn't happen back then? Hardly. It's been around since the fall of man. If your more takes you to people you don't like for whatever reason, don't be a Jonah. Don't let your dislike about a group of people or a person tarnish your more. Who are you to argue with God?

Jonah's story: the book of Jonah in the Old Testament.

Haman

Haman was not Jewish. He probably believed in many gods. I include his story, though, because Haman plays a significant role when you later read about Esther. Haman's story shows how God may use someone outside our faith to propel us to our purpose. The stories of Esther and Haman overlap but from different perspectives. You can read their stories in the short book of Esther in the Bible.

There are many lessons we can learn from Haman. He is one of my favorite villains in Scripture (Is that a terrible thing to say?) because you can see the steps to his downfall from the beginning. Haven't you ever known someone who continually makes poor decisions? You see where their decisions are taking them, and it's not good? In this story, you want to yell, "Haman, stop! You are going to cause your own demise."

We can see Haman is a man full of himself. He wants him and the king to be "besties." He hates the Israelites, but one in particular, which you will learn about shortly. The king elevates Haman, giving him a seat of honor higher than all the other nobles. Haman was flying high, so the king had ordered all the royal officials at the king's gate to kneel and honor Haman. Esther 3:2: ".... but Mordecai would not kneel or pay him honor."

Mordecai worships God, and Haman sees this as defiance. "When Haman saw that Mordecai would not kneel down or pay him honor, he was outraged." (Esther 3:5). I don't even think it's because Mordecai is Jewish, as much as the lack of reverence that Haman feels Mordecai displays towards him. Haman admits that the only thing (or so Haman thinks) keeping him from being happy is Mordecai's lack of reverence for him. He is furious.

Bragging to his wife and friends, he states: "Even Esther the queen let no one, but me come with the king to the banquet which she had prepared: and tomorrow also, I am invited by her with the King. Yet all of this does not satisfy me every time I see Mordecai the Jew sitting at the king's gate." (Esther 5: 13-14).

It is like most of us to read a statement like the one above and say, "What a jerk!" Seriously, who would let just one thing ruin their life? Most of us probably think we would never be like Haman. I mean, we aren't expecting anyone to bow down to us?

Or are we?

Some of us want everyone to look up to us. We want to be admired and considered important. We might not say that out loud, but if people decided to put us on a pedestal, we wouldn't say no. But a pedestal, because of its very design, tall and narrow, is easily knocked over.

I recently watched a really old movie called Forever Amber. While I ate my popcorn and watched the heroine, I just wanted to reach into the TV screen and yell at her, "This will not work out the way you think!" Alas, it didn't either. She lost everything. Watching her character make the decisions she did was like watching an oncoming train wreck.

You can see the train wreck coming, but you can do nothing about it except pray. I hate writing it that way because prayer is the absolute best thing we can do, but I think you know what I'm saying. Watching someone heading down the wrong path toward a disastrous ending is heartbreaking. We see the end of their movie and know their hearts will be broken if they don't change course.

Inside, we are no different from Haman. Whether or not we admit it, we all want to feel special. And there's nothing wrong with feeling special. But when it requires the undying admiration of other people, especially just one person, it isn't feeling special that is our goal: it's worship.

I have a blog, **goodthoughtsgoodlives.com.** That wasn't the original title. The very first title was "The worm in my apple." Many people think that if it weren't for that one thing, that one annoying worm, they would be happy, prosperous, or whatever. Well, for Haman, Mordecai was the worm in his apple.

He is so obsessed with Mordecai's behavior that he is eaten alive with hatred and jealousy. Not only does he plot Mordecai's death, but the entire Israelite population! That's hatred on a whole other level. Sounds a bit like Jonah, doesn't he?

And, before we get too smug, think about some people's attitudes today. They have a terrible encounter with a person of a different race and end up hating them all. Throughout history, unfounded hatred has been responsible for eradicating various ethnic groups. The world has not evolved all that much from Haman's time. God forbid any Christians today think like Haman did. Watch out. The train is coming!

Haman endures a humiliating experience before the king decides to hang him. The king is having a sleepless night, so he looks over some old records. The king reads that sometime earlier, Mordecai had foiled an assassination attempt on the king. The king realizes he hasn't honored Mordecai for that act of bravery and wants to make it right now.

He tells Haman that he, Haman, will place a regal robe on this person and lead the horse with the honored man on it down the street while shouting out his praise. He has no idea who this man is, and can you imagine the humiliation when Haman learns this man is Mordecai?

Haman lives through the ordeal. Later, Esther has a couple of banquets to which she invites Haman with a plan to expose him. Haman is puffed up over this and tells his friends and family that the Queen has specially chosen him to attend her banquets.

In the meantime, Haman has devised a plan to have all the Jews killed. During the second dinner, Esther exposes Mordecai's plan to kill her and her people. The king is so enraged that he leaves for the palace garden to think about what to do next. He now knows that Esther is Jewish as well.

Haman is terrified that the king knows his plan. He falls on the couch before Esther and pleads for his life. The king returns to the room, and as he views the scene from his perspective, it looks like Haman is molesting Esther.

He immediately arrests Haman and orders him to be hanged. (You have to read the book of Esther.) And guess whose gallows they hang him on?

The very ones he prepared for Mordecai! Talk about "what goes around, comes around." Haman wanted "more," the wrong kind of "more." God does not stamp his approval on a wrong more, but God can use someone's wrong more to lead us to our right more. God used Haman's bad choices and ill-intents to open the door for Esther's more to emerge.

How often have people turned their lives around despite the evil that surrounded or forced on them? Sometimes, great programs start because God uses the evil in this world to prompt Christians to seek their purpose, like MADD Mothers Against Drunk Driving.

Haman's story: Book of Esther in the Old Testament.

Judas

And that takes us to Judas and his tragic story. I have great empathy for Judas. I believe he was a loner among the disciples. Picture a man who desperately wanted to be a part of this group but never felt like he was. I picture him as that person we all know who never fits in but never really tries, either. I read this statement below a while ago, and it's so true. It goes something like this:

"Don't complain that you're not part of the group when you've been hanging out on the fringe."

I believe that describes Judas. There is no account of Judas being "one of the guys." With the other disciples, you get the idea that they hung out together and had healthy, if not perfect, relationships with each other. But nothing indicates Judas was part of the inner circle.

Judas appears to be a fringe-dweller. He didn't seem to pal around with the disciples. Maybe his profession was the issue with them. But you never read his name connected with the disciples in a good way. And even though his story was written after he betrayed Jesus, you would think someone would've written about it if there had been something good to say.

His financial greediness was apparent. Judas complained about the expensive oil Mary used to anoint the feet of Jesus and said they could have given it to the poor. But that was a lie, as the Bible states: "Now, he (Judas) said this not because he was concerned about the poor, but because he was a thief, and as he had the money box, he used to pilfer what was put into it." Judas was already a thief. John (12: 5-6.)

Then there is Matthew, another disciple. Mathew's former occupation was that of a tax collector. Considering his former profession, I wonder why he wasn't given the treasurer's job. I would guess that Matthew watched Judas carefully. Did he notice something? If Matthew saw something suspicious, did he tell Jesus? Some unanswered questions for sure, but back to Judas.

Think about it. Jesus had handpicked Judas to be a disciple! What an honor. Judas walked and talked with Jesus. He had companionship with Jesus. What went wrong? But then, what goes wrong with us at times? We, too, walk and talk with Jesus and even have the Bible and the Holy Spirit, which the disciples didn't in the beginning, and yet we also make mistakes.

Judas betrayed Jesus for thirty pieces of silver. In Exodus, we learn that if an animal gores a slave to death, the animal's owner must pay 30 shekels for the loss of the slave. From this perspective, we can say that Jesus' death equaled that of a slave, which seems fitting because Jesus was servant-God.

Judas goes to the chief priests and offers to deliver Jesus to them for thirty pieces of silver, the time and place to be determined. Judas looks for the right opportunity. It comes at night when the most evil happens. Judas leads them to Jesus in the garden of Gethsemane right after Jesus has finished praying his prayer of torment and acceptance. Judas betrays Jesus with a kiss, which he has already indicated would be the sign to identify Christ. Think about that for a moment. A kiss! (Mark 14:45)

Judas didn't necessarily believe his betrayal would have the consequences that it did. He probably thought there would be a trial, and that would be it. Jesus would be released. Or better yet, perform some miraculous feat. The Bible states Judas felt remorse. (Matthew 27:3-5) What it doesn't say is remorse about what? Because his plan had backfired? Remorse because of what he did to Jesus? I will give him the benefit of the doubt and suggest he might have felt remorse because Judas does try to return the money, hoping they would change their mind. But, of course, they didn't.

Perhaps Judas had planned to tell Jesus what he'd done after he got his money back. Money was more important to Judas than the life of his Savior and Lord. Instead of trying to find Jesus to beg for forgiveness, Judas hung himself. He never understood Jesus's messages about forgiveness. What a tragedy.

Neither Matthew nor Mark wrote about Judas's suicide in their book. Did they know he recanted and tried to change things? I doubt it. I believe if they had, they would have, for Jesus' sake, tried to help him make a different decision. But, again, Judas had remained at the fringes.

What did the priests do? They recognized the thirty pieces of silver as blood money and used it to buy a plot at Potter's field, a burial place for strangers. But Judas dug his own grave much earlier. You can read about Judas in Matthew \26 and 27: 1-10.

There are always tragedies when we throw away the more God has given us. When we turn our back on our purpose, our mission, there is only despair. Lot, Jonah, Haman, and Judas are examples *not* to follow but to *learn* from. The next chapter will examine the other mores, beginning with the right ones.

Judas's story: Matthew 10:4, Luke 22:3, John 6:71, 13:29, 18:2, Luke 16:6, Acts 1:15-26, all in New Testament.

SEVEN: THE RIGHT MORES

Once again, right mores are always God-initiated, God-honoring, and for the good of others. While we may profit in some way, that is not the goal.

I will use examples of Noah, Joseph, Ruth, and Daniel. Their mores fit the definition. But that doesn't mean every step of the way was clear, easy, or without its struggles.

Noah

There is an old song with these words, "Noah found grace in the eyes of the LORD," based on the verse in Genesis 6:8. Noah was the only righteous man on the earth. Think about that. The only righteous person on earth. That's something when you think about it.

Ironically, the name Noah derives from the Hebrew word to mean "rest." Building an ark and surviving a flood doesn't sound much like rest, does it? In Genesis 6:7, God looks at the earth and its inhabitants and sees how corrupt man has become. He decides to eliminate all of them. This action is hard to understand, but we should remember that God's knowledge far exceeds ours, and we don't know the extent of the evil prevalent in Noah's day.

But God has not decided to completely wipe out humankind and start with another type of Adam and Eve. He has watched his servant Noah and knows him to be righteous, so God decides he will repopulate the earth through Noah's line.

My husband and I visited The Ark exhibit in Kentucky three years ago, which was eye-opening. Not only was Noah an obedient servant, but he was also almost a genius. The complexities of the ark's design are hard to believe. How Noah knew to build it the way he did is amazing. The ecology in the ark is stupefying.

But what might even be more so is Noah's faithfulness amid the taunts, ridicule, etc. It took years to build the ark. And remember, he built the ark in an arid land. He had no idea what a flood was, having never seen rain. And to construct an enormous building that would float on water? It's mind-boggling. But Noah, like Daniel, *made up his mind to be faithful.*

Can you imagine the scorn and ridicule Noah must have endured year after year? I think most of us would've given up. Maybe that's why I told only a few people when my first book was done and ready to be published. I might have caved had I run into ridicule and scorn.

I would love to talk to Noah and ask him how he survived the scorn and ridicule of his neighbors. How did he respond when God told him he and his family were the only people to survive the flood? Did he believe God would destroy all the people on the earth except for Noah and his family?

And when God gives him the blueprints. How did he even understand them? And the size? It's a shame we don't give Noah the time we give other heroes of the Bible. We think, "Noah. Yea, he's the one who built the ark." We never think about what that must have been like. How overwhelming it must have been. And yet Noah never capitulates. Amazing.

Do you realize that God even told Noah his detailed plans? Not just about how to build the ark but also about his future. Noah stands with Abraham in that regard.

Have you ever wondered if you'd like to know God's plans for you and your loved ones? I think most of us would say "no." There's only so much foreknowledge we want. But could there be people today to whom God has revealed the future? I'm only asking. I don't know whether there is or not. Back to the shipbuilding.

Genesis 7:5 states, "And Noah did all that the LORD commanded him." Not some of it or even most of it. All of it. I wish I could say I do everything God tells me to do. Noah was six hundred years old when he finished the ark. Even though we know the life spans were much longer in Biblical times, Noah was well-advanced even in Biblical years.

God makes a covenant with Noah to never destroy the world again through a flood. The covenant made with Noah is one of only four covenants God made with an individual or nation in the Old Testament. The other three covenants were made with Abraham, Israel, and David. Noah was the first.

Of all the Biblical examples, I know of only two that never slipped once in their obedience: Noah and Daniel. (Jesus, of course, but that should be obvious.)

Also, I cannot think of another example who, when given their more, followed it right down to the letter. But because Noah was so righteous and faithful, I think it's fair to say he always sought God's will. His more was the result of his daily walk with God.

And unlike so many of us, were we given such a vast more, Noah never dropped a beat. There wasn't a nail left unfixed, a crack left unpitched, an angle that was not honed to perfection. We often place Noah *only* within the story of the Ark and the Flood. However, the story is much more about Noah and his faithfulness.

Faithfulness matters to God, and it always leads to more.

Jonah's story: Book of Jonah, the Old Testament.

Joseph

Joseph is our next example of someone who found his more while living his life, although in this case, others were in charge of it for a while. The story of Joseph is long, so I will try to condense it as much as possible while remaining true to the story. I will have to leave out many details, but you can read the complete account in Genesis 30-37.

First, Joseph, like Jacob, was a favored child. Joseph's father loved him more than the others because Joseph was Rachel's son, the woman he loved and worked for fourteen years for. (Jacob's account is told in the Detoured Mores chapter.)

Many scholars believe Joseph was a spoiled teenager. I don't necessarily think that. Yes, Joseph should have kept some things to himself, like his dreams, especially those of his brothers bowing down to him. That was ill-advised.

His older brothers were already jealous of him anyway. Instead of understanding this was the dream of their seventeen-year-old younger brother, who was probably trying to get their attention, they took offense. But the dream offended even his father, Jacob. I think the brothers were looking for a reason to hate Joseph. They teased him, calling him "The Dreamer."

On another occasion, Jacob sends Joseph out to check on Joseph's brothers. Joseph is wearing a one-of-a-kind, multi-colored coat. Sending Joseph to check on them and wearing the special coat his father made for him is the last straw. The brothers have had it with Joseph being lorded over them. And that coat! Enough is enough. They decide to kill him, but one brother, Reuben, jumps in and says, "No," let's throw him in the pit instead, which they do. And then they sit down to eat! Seriously, that's what they did. Joseph is in a pit, possibly hurt, and they eat their lunch!

The despicable brothers spot a caravan of merchants on the horizon. Judah, another brother who does not want Joseph harmed, gets an idea. He suggests they sell him to the traders. Reuben, another brother, is unaware of this, and when Rueben goes to rescue Joseph, he finds he is gone. Because Reuben is the eldest brother, he knows his father will hold him responsible. So he suggests they kill an animal, take Joseph's coat, dip it in the blood, and tell their father a wild animal killed him. It's a pretty clever scheme.

In the meantime, the traders sell Joseph to King Potiphar. Many things have happened over the years, but I will move right past them and get to what I think is the best part of the story because it contains one of the most beloved verses in all scripture.

Joseph survives a false rape claim against him by Potiphar's wife and eventually becomes the manager of all of the king's holdings. Joseph now ranks second only to the king and has become a very wealthy man himself.

He predicts a famine in Egypt and, in preparation, comes up with a brilliant plan. During the years of plenty, he stores up grain in advance. The famine hits, and the people cry out to Pharoah, and he tells them, "Go see Joseph." They do, and Joseph opens the grain storehouses and sells the grain to anyone who wants it.

In the meantime, Joseph's father, his sons, and their families suffer from widespread famine. The Bible states that the famine was severe in all the land, extending beyond Egypt. It affected Canaan as well, which is where Joseph's family lived. They learn that a ruler in Egypt is selling grain, and Jacob asks his sons, "What are you waiting for? Go buy some grain."

And, of course, they have to buy from the manager for Potiphar's affairs, although they have no idea it is their brother. It has been years since they've seen him, and for all they know, he is dead or in some faraway land. When they do see him, they don't recognize him at all, although he certainly does them.

Intriguing events happen over the following few chapters. Talk about drama and unexpected twists! But finally, Joseph reveals his true identity to his brothers. Of course, they expect to be killed on the spot. But Joseph doesn't. Instead, he forgives them, and they are greatly relieved. Joseph reunites with his father.

Jacob is very old by now, and he dies. The brothers are anxious and ask, "What if Joseph bears a grudge against us and pays us back in full for the wrong we did now that our father has died?" Instead of running away, they come to Joseph voluntarily, falling down before him, and offer their allegiance. In other words, they beg for their lives. Their willingness to face Joseph is one of the few good things we can say about them in this scenario.

Then Joseph delivers these beautiful words as only a truly righteous man who has remained righteous his entire life can say.

"As for you, you meant evil against me, but God meant it for good in order to bring about this present result, to preserve many people alive." (Genesis 50:20)

(As a side note, these brothers are the twelve tribes of Israel. Can you understand then why the Israelites suffer a heap of trouble? They aren't exactly stellar examples of leadership.)

Joseph always made the right decisions. I excuse what a seventeen-year-old man might have said to get his brothers' attention. Joseph was a man of integrity. After his capture, he made a series of right managerial choices. Those choices saved thousands of lives.

His brothers threw him into a pit. Traders sold him like a slave. He was imprisoned. But God had a plan. Read that again.

God had a plan.

God still has plans.

When we are in our lowest pit, God still has plans for us. It may not look like Joseph's. We will probably not gain the fame or wealth Joseph did, although, of course, all things are possible with God.

But God has more for us that is just as important in God's eyes and his overall plan for the world. The God of all that we see, the God of eternity, is waiting to give us our more as well.

Had Joseph not followed his more, many people would have died. The twelve nations of Israel might never have come into existence.

When we realize what our more is, it might be pretty challenging to get there. Just because we've identified and labeled it doesn't mean it is clear sailing. But we must preserve and remember what Thomas Edison said, "Success is 10 percent inspiration and 90% perspiration".

Joesph's story: Genesis, chapters 37, 39-50.

Ruth

Ruth, by the book of the same name, is another example of a right more. Here's some of the backstory for you.

Ruth was married to the son of a woman named Naomi. Because of a famine, Naomi, her husband, Elimelech, and two sons left Bethlehem and traveled to Moab. Moabites worshipped false gods. While there, Elimelech dies and leaves Naomi to raise her two sons, Mahlon and Chilion. When the time was right for them to get married, they married women who were Moabites, of which Ruth was one. Although not explicitly forbidden, this practice was not approved under Mosaic law. The wives' names were Orpah and Ruth.

Both young husbands, Naomi's sons, die. Naomi decides to return to Bethlehem, where she has family and friends. Somewhere along the journey, Naomi tells her daughters-in-law to leave. After all, she explains, I have no more sons to marry you. You have no chance to have children. Leave me and go your way if you want any kind of life.

Initially, they both assure her they will stay with her, but Orpah finally leaves. There is much crying and clinging at this point. The three women loved each other dearly. What a model for daughters-in-law and mothers-in-law.

I know many such loving relationships. It is not grounds for "mother-in-law" jokes, as many would believe. My experience with my daughter-in-law is such an example, as was my daughter's relationship with her mother-in-law. I know more of those healthy relationships than those joked about so often.

Once more, Naomi tries to get Ruth to go back, but Ruth replies with these most famous words: "Wherever you go, I will go. Your people will be my people, and your God, my God."

This statement shows Ruth has turned away from worshipping false gods and is now worshipping the one true God. God is in control of this situation, as you will soon see. Naomi realizes she can't change Ruth's mind. So, they continue their journey and arrive in Bethlehem right after the barley harvest.

The two women, without husbands to support them, are having a rough time financially. Ruth asks permission to go to the field of Boaz, a relative of Naomi's former husband, to pick up what they left over after the gleaners have gone through, which was a common practice. Boaz spots her, learns who she is, that her mother-in-law is Naomi, and instructs his workers to always leave something extra behind for her.

One day, Ruth is resting in the shelter provided for the workers. Boaz tells her that he has not only instructed the gleaners to purposely leave her extra grain but also that she is safe from any uninvited male advances. He tells her she can drink from his servant's water jars and even shares a meal with her.

It astounded Ruth that this man is kind to her, and she asks him why. Boaz responds he has heard what she did for Naomi. (Forgive me, but I can't help but say this is an excellent example of reaping and sowing. Ruth sowed kindness to Naomi, and she reaped through the kindness of Boaz.) Boaz is smitten with Ruth but knows there is a relative who is closer in relationship to her than he. According to the tradition of the time, Boaz has to give that person the first choice to marry Ruth. In the meantime, Naomi still has the land from her husband's estate, but she has to sell it to provide for herself and Ruth. Boaz is in charge of the sale.

Boaz tells the first-choice relative about the land deal and allows him an opportunity to buy it. The relative agrees. However, when he learns Ruth comes with the bargain, he backs out because it would increase his financial responsibilities to care for two more women (Naomi and Ruth would be part of the arrangement.). He has his own family to care for. The man offers the land back to Boaz, and Boaz buys it. The elders confirmed the deal and blessed Boaz: "May the LORD make the woman who is coming into your home like Rachel and Leah, both of whom built the house of Israel."

But our God is a God of more, and not only does Ruth bear a child who brings life back to Naomi, but there is also this.

Ruth 4:17: "... so they named him Obed. **He is the father of Jesse, the father of David."**

Jesus is from the house of David, so Jesus was Ruth's direct descendant. Is that a more or what?

The book of Ruth is only four chapters long, so I hope you will read it. Ruth does what I suggest in the how-to section of this book. She quietly lives her life, making good choices right along. She meets and marries Boaz. They have a son, and her genealogy includes our Savior.

I could've placed Ruth's story under detoured mores, but I included it here because it is such an excellent example of a right more. There are few people in the Bible for whom nothing negative is written about them. Ruth is another example. Her kindness to Naomi is something we all should aspire to.

How we treat people matters.

Ruth's story: Book of Ruth in the Old Testament.

Daniel

Daniel is one of my Old Testament heroes. One of my favorite verses is, "But Daniel made up his mind...." Daniel 1:8. I love what a determined young man Daniel was. He was intentional (a word I dearly love.) From the moment of his captivity, he was faithful to the God of his youth. Nothing anyone did steered him away from his beliefs for one moment, *throughout his entire life.* That can't be said for most of us.

Here's a quick recap if you need it. Daniel was taken into slavery when he was young because King Nebuchadnezzar, king of Babylon, had captured the Israelites in Jerusalem and brought them to Babylon. Nebuchadnezzar ordered his chief official to identify some intelligent, good-looking young men with no physical defects and bring them into the king's service. Daniel was one of those young men. The king further ordered that they be schooled for three years in the language and the culture, after which they would enter the king's service.

The king also ordered the boys to eat a specific diet consisting of the king's choice of food. I would guess that would mean it was a rich and calorie-laden diet consisting of the finest meats, wine, and all forms of sweet cakes and bread. Yum.

Whether the king thought the young men were too thin or not, we don't know. But *Daniel made up his mind* (Again, I love that) that he wouldn't do that. He felt it would defile him because the meat hadn't been slain per the Mosaic law. There was also the fact that the food and wine had been offered to pagan gods. Daniel tells the king's emissary that he would like to counter the king's proposal. When you think about it, that alone was pretty brave. Daniel easily could have been executed for that suggestion.

But God paved the way for Daniel and his friends. Daniel suggests the king allow him and his friends to eat fruits and veggies instead and evaluate their health in a few weeks to see how healthy they are. The king agrees. In a few weeks, they are deemed healthy, and the king agrees to let them continue to eat the way they always have.

What's the big deal, you say? Why not just eat what the king offered? A few weeks wouldn't have made that much of a difference. But the food was not the issue. Maybe the phrase, "It's the principle that counts," came from this incident. It certainly fits. Daniel, as a Jew, was brought up to follow specific rules about what foods he could or couldn't eat and how the food was prepared. He would have been going against everything he believed in had he given in. He chose integrity.

Oh, that we would all make up our minds about so many tempting issues in our lives. The right more will always refuse to compromise. It will always put faith in God first.

A lot happens in Daniel's life, but we need to get to the lion's den because that is what most people think about when they hear the name Daniel. Years have transpired, and Darius is now the king. Daniel has gained an excellent reputation over the years, and King Darius names him a commissioner. He excels so much that the king makes plans to give him reign over his entire kingdom. There was competition for the job, but Daniel was a shoo-in unless somebody could find something against him.

The opposition knew Daniel was faithful to his God. They knew he prayed to his God three times a day. So, they devised a brilliant plan. They talked the king into signing an injunction, and here's the critical part: an injunction based on the law of the Medes and Persians. According to that law, even the king himself could not revoke it once signed. Period. The injunction read that no man could pray to any God or man besides the king for thirty days.

Naturally, after this clever ploy, they tell the king that Daniel is not obeying and is praying and petitioning his own God. These conspirators knew the king could not revoke this law no matter how much he liked Daniel. The king was distraught to learn this and even tried to devise a plan to rescue Daniel. But the cohort of jealous men reminded the king he could not go against the law of the Medes and Persians; he had to follow through.

The king's men threw Daniel into the lion's den. The king didn't sleep at all that night. At the break of dawn, he went to the lion's den. He yelled down into the pit, *"Daniel, servant of the living God, has your God whom you **constantly** serve been able to deliver you from the lion's den"*?

The king was thrilled when Daniel answered that he was OK

and that there wasn't even a scratch on him. The king ordered the malicious men who contrived the scheme and their families to be thrown into that same lion's den. (Sounds a bit like the Haman story.) They were all killed. After that, King Darius made a decree that in all his kingdom, men were to fear and tremble before the God of Daniel. (Read the entire proclamation in Daniel 6: 26-28.)

Daniel experiences much throughout his life. Angels visit him. He experiences frightening visions of the future. He writes, "... my thoughts were greatly alarming me, and my face grew pale, but I kept them to myself." (Daniel 5:6)

Daniel is another example in the Bible in which no negative word is written. He is the truest example of someone whose purpose, whose more, was clear from the beginning and never wavered. Not for one minute.

I could've used the example of Daniel in the chapter about detoured mores because it would certainly fit. Daniel was undoubtedly detoured. He was ripped from his family, taken to a foreign land, and told to worship the king instead of his God. But he never wavers, and the book ends with Daniel in conversation with an angel, not his first angel encounter, I should add.

We learn from Daniel that our more doesn't depend on our age or circumstances. The book of Daniel is an exclamation point for a man who lived out his more in every sense of the word, from what he did or didn't eat to whom he did or didn't serve.

Daniel stood up for what he believed. Nothing caused him to

turn away from God, not even a lion's den. And let's face it; we are all in a lion's den at one time or another. We've all been in that place where we feel we will be devoured. We have a choice then. Trust God or be eaten alive. "... but Daniel decided."

Daniel's story: Book of Daniel in the Old Testament.

EIGHT: DETOURED MORES

Sometimes, we know our more, but we get detoured. Some of the reasons for our detour may be outside our control. Illness in the family can side-track us, as can unemployment, a physical move, or a job change. Many circumstances can conspire together to set us back for a time. That can be hard. We've found our purpose, our more, and now we feel stuck. We've taken a detour.

But maybe a detour is needed. Perhaps we need more education or better skills. Maybe we need to bring other people on board. No matter the reason, it's hard to know your more and then feel you've delegated to the back burner. My first book wasn't published until last year because I felt side-tracked due to my mom's illness and the events surrounding her care.

But we mustn't use detours as an excuse. It's easy to let discouragement or time restrictions get the best of us. But we can do all we can until the path is clear again. We can learn, research, practice current skills, and learn new ones.

A detour doesn't have to be permanent. Maybe we are side-lined because God knows the timing of our more isn't quite right. Can't God reveal our more and simultaneously put it on hold? Yes. Maybe he sees something in our future that, were we to rush ahead, would compromise our more.

For example, I felt compelled to write a book many years before the book was published. I look back and see that certain things must be in place first. I kept working on it, anyway, knowing the time wasn't right. I started a blog. After certain events, I knew it was time to finish and publish the book.

I think of a couple building a house. They're excited. It's a lifelong dream. But then they run into all kinds of issues. The contractor says there are serious foundation issues he had not expected. The couple doesn't understand the seriousness, but the contractor tells them that to proceed would be folly. They are frustrated, and confused and wonder if they should insist the contractor continues or hire a contractor that tells them what they want to hear. But they don't. Eventually, the building starts again; they move into their home only to find out later that those issues, had they built anyway, would've meant an unsafe house.

There are two types of detours or side-lines. One is when we detour ourselves, and the other is when circumstances or other people detour us. And I suppose there are times they happen simultaneously. It is important to remember that detours and sidelines can be redirected. Sometimes, we may have to retrace our steps, but at other times, we might have to take a new path. But the outcome is the same; we get to where we need to be.

I didn't think twice about deciding who would be my first example of a detoured more. I can think of no more straightforward example than the Israelites wandering in the desert for forty years.

Israelites

Most people think their forty-year journey began when they

left Egypt. It didn't. They got to the border of the promised land the year before the wandering began. Here's that story.

Twelve spies representing each of the twelve tribes of Israel are sent out to survey the land and come back with a report. Ten spies said there were "giants" living in the land and they should turn around because they would not win a battle with them. But two of the spies, young men named Caleb and Joshua, said, "If God is on our side, we can win. Don't be afraid. Let's go get 'em!" The Israelites didn't want to hear that and tried to stone Caleb and Joshua.

The Israelites listened to their fear. They listened to the ten naysayers. Because of their fear, they begin to walk in circles. (Numbers 14:34.) If God had said, "Don't worry, you won't have to fight; I'll just hand them over," they would probably have marched right in. But instead, God tells them they will wander in the desert for forty years, one year for each day the spies were out.

Think about it. The Israelites were literally at the edge of the Promised land when they were commanded to turn around. Of that generation, only Joshua and Caleb entered the promised land; the rest died out as God said they would (Numbers 14: 27-35).

The very next morning, after God announced they would wander in the desert for forty years, some Israelites recanted. They said, *We didn't mean what we said. Forget about it. We will enter the promised land just like God said we should.* Moses tries to warn them, saying, "the LORD isn't with you now.

They will kill you. Don't go.." They foolishly go ahead anyway. The enemy attacked them, and many Israelites died.

As an aside, the number forty in scripture is the most interesting. It rained forty and forty nights during The Flood. Moses was forty years old when he killed the Egyptian and fled to the desert, where he earned a living as a shepherd for forty years. The forty years of wandering matched the forty days the spies scoped out Canaan. Moses spent forty days on Mount Sinai receiving the Ten Commandments. (Acts 7:23-36) Jesus was tempted in the wilderness for forty days. There were forty days between the resurrection and the ascension. There is no particular message here, and we probably shouldn't look for one. But I find it interesting.

It's impossible to recount the entire wilderness story here, but their journey is fraught with many problems. You'll have to read the book of Exodus. And it's good to read it in one setting to get the whole gist of the story. It won't take that long, and you probably spend that much time reading other things anyway, so give it a shot.

I often use the Israelites as an example of how *not* to do things, but I'm not much different. I, too, complain of sore feet and other things. I don't trust enough and don't always want to take leaps of faith. The Israelites, to a degree, represent all of us.

Let's return to their escape from Egypt and the exciting parting of the Red Sea. The Red Sea crossing happens *before* their wilderness journey begins. I can imagine those first few days after the crossing were filled with excitement at the thought of a "land flowing with milk and honey." According to one source, it would've taken twenty-five days for the first group to reach the Red Sea after leaving Egypt. Because there were so many of them, it took some time for them to all cross. So far, so good.

We don't have to imagine how they acted afterward because Exodus fifteen tells us they were all singing praise to God. But they sing a different tune only three days into their journey. Remember, this is three days just after the last of them have experienced walking on dry land in the middle of the Red Sea.

They arrive at the Desert of Shur planning on fresh water, but it is too bitter to drink, so they grumble to Moses. Moses performs a miracle, and the water becomes good to drink. Coming up are some famous words that we don't hear quoted too often.

On only the fifteenth day of the *second* month, after they had left Egypt, the Israelites complained again about the food. The Israelites even claim they had eaten as much as they wanted when they were in captivity, "Would that we had died by the LORD'S hand and in the land of Egypt when we sat by the pot of meat when we ate bread to the full."

It wasn't even true! They had been beaten and starved under Egyptian rule. Discontent in the present can undoubtedly distort and glorify the past. But that's what happens when you grumble. Your memory goes awry. And it had only been two months since they were enslaved! How quickly they forgot.

I could go on and on.

After escaping all the plagues inflicted on the Egyptians, the Israelites probably thought the journey to the promised land would be easy, certainly better than the life they knew. Otherwise, why leave in the first place? I guess they assumed that because God had performed such amazing wonders, he would continue to do so for the entire trip.

If you've ever struggled with depression or anxiety, you know how it feels when you are getting better. You assume your depression will continue waning until it doesn't. We almost always experience healing from depression like a roller-coaster ride, up, down, and all around. There is more work to be done. There are thoughts, words, habits that need changing, and a heart that needs healing. It takes time. (See my book, *Depression Has a Big Voice. Make Yours Bigger!* For more information, visit https://goodthoughtsgoodlives.com).

The Israelites complained when confronted with the first challenge, the bitter water. Then it was the food. Then it was this, and then it was that. And with each challenge, you see their coming demise. The Israelites completely lost the joy of their exodus from Egypt. Is it any wonder that when confronted with the reports of the spies, they believed the ten who gave a discouraging report instead of the two who said, "Hey, we can do it?" They had already lost the vision of their more. Otherwise, they would've entered the promised land on schedule. Look at a map of their journey. You will be astounded.

God not only rescued the Israelites but had another more for them as well, a land flowing with milk and honey. A haven for them. A rest for them. But it was going to take forty years to get there. We don't want to use them as an example to follow, now, do we?

There is a lesson we can learn from this detour. Don't give up on the first hardship. Discouragement causes many people to fail to accomplish their more. Discouragement is a real goal-stopper. I know.

When I realized God was directing me to write a book, I got so discouraged so often that I'm ashamed to admit it. That's how bad it was. There were days I wanted to delete every word I wrote. I was overwhelmed. Thank goodness God did not give up on me, and now this second book has been published.

I think of a runner anticipating running his first marathon only to suffer a foot injury. He misses his marathon. The doctor tells him that had he run anyway, which he almost did, he would've damaged his foot beyond repair. He recuperates and starts training all over again, and when he runs his first marathon, his time is better than ever. I'm sure we can all think of times when we've been sidelined, only to discover later that it was the best thing to have happened.

If our relationship with God is where it should be, we can trust that our detoured more will always get back on track. It's hard to know your purpose and then feel like it will never come to fruition. If there are legitimate reasons, *we* must put our more on hold; God will not take away our more. As suggested, more may be required before achieving our purpose successfully. We must be careful not to forge ahead when there are clear signs we need more preparation. But when there is a clear sign we *should* move forward, we must also do that. Interestingly, advance preparation may even streamline the process.

A detoured more can be thrown away if we are not careful. So how does that happen?

<u>First</u> of all, we don't trust God. We don't believe he will continue to direct us when we're stalled. We doubt our original call.

<u>Second</u>, fear detours us. We look at the battle ahead, and just like the Israelites, we run away. **Fear is doubt on steroids.** When fear takes over, we can't, no, we won't, take the next step.

<u>Third,</u> we listen to other people.

I learned long ago that when God has revealed a special message to us, we keep it to ourselves. Not forever, but until the message has simmered in our hearts and souls. You need time for reflection and prayer. Then you can share it with a few close somebodies, but not a lot of everybodies. Here's why.

It's the same reason most artists keep their work hidden until it's ready to be shown. Non-artists don't understand the process of painting a picture. Consequently, because they don't have the vision of the final painting that the artist does, they are quick to judge.

When I started writing my book, only my husband knew about it. Other people knew I was writing but didn't know the subject matter. They didn't know how far I was into the process and didn't know it would culminate in a book. I wanted to relish this call from God and enjoy it as unique. It was from God to me. Like Paul, I felt I had to be in my own Arabia and unavailable for a time. I continue to keep my writing under wraps until I've edited my book at least once.

The Israelites are only one example. We all know someone who has been "detoured" because of poor personal decisions. We probably saw it coming. We may have even addressed it. But until that person realizes on their own that they have taken a detour, no amount of coercing can turn them around. They will have to learn from their mistakes, and like God watched the Israelites learn from theirs, it will break our hearts.

Someone is reading this and saying, "But what if you're not the one who took the detour? What if you were forced to take a wrong path?"

God never disciplines us for other people's wrong actions. And nothing can stop God's plan for our lives when we follow God. It may take longer; it may look different. But no forced detour can thwart God's more for us.

As we walk in his will and pursue the work God has placed before us, we will find ourselves back on track. Even though we've waylaid, we are stronger and more capable now. It could be that had we not been detoured, we wouldn't be able to fast-track now.

I felt that way when I was writing my first book. My mother's illness put things on hold for me for several years. I had been writing and feeling clear about my direction when I had to step back. I look back now and realize I couldn't have written that first book or this one had that detour not happened. I had too much to learn. Now, when I sit down to write, I write at warp speed because I'm not wading through a lot of mental "stuff."

So don't get discouraged if you've been on a detour that wasn't by your hands. God is so amazing. We only have to draw near him, and he will get us back on track. He will remove the detour and open the road again. It may be a quick detour or a long detour, but remember, God created your map in the first place.

But if you detour yourself, are lost, and don't know which road to take to get back to where you got off, guess what? You don't have to. God only wants you to acknowledge your mistake, ask for forgiveness, seek his guidance, and he will set your feet on the right path once again.

God is the most loving parent you can imagine. We can't comprehend it because none of us can love like him. Thank goodness we don't have to. We would fail miserably. It's all on him, and that's precisely how he wants it.

The Old Testament is about the Israelites' story, but reading only the book Exodus will tell you a lot.

Israelites' story: the Old Testament.

Jacob

If ever there was an obvious detoured more, it's the story of Jacob. And if there were ever a man whose life I don't get, it's Jacob. (Jacob's name means "deceiver.") God had a more for

Jacob. Why Jacob? I don't have the slightest idea. He doesn't seem like a stellar individual to me. God's more for Jacob is a big more because Jacob's sons will become the twelve tribes of Israel. That is huge. Let's look at Jacob's story.

One day, Jacob cooked a delicious stew when his twin brother, Esau, came in from working in the fields, and he was famished. He asked Jacob for some stew. And clever Jacob, knowing one could barter for a birthright, told his brother, "You can have some stew if you give me your birthright." That meant Esau, his minutes- older twin brother, would no longer have precedence over his younger brother or be assured a double inheritance. Esau is so hungry and seemingly cares so little for the birthright that he agrees.

Esau gave up a spiritual blessing for a bowl of stew. Jacob used Esau's hunger against him to get what he wanted. They are both in the wrong. By the way, Esau has already shown he wasn't interested in spiritual things, having married two idol-worshipping women earlier in his life, so this little incident shouldn't raise any eyebrows. Esau was already heading down the wrong path.

While Jacob, according to Jewish law, could barter for a birthright, it certainly doesn't speak well for him. It would be like your brother or sister who is starving. You have a pot of stew on the stove, but you won't give them any until they give you something, like maybe their inheritance, before you feed them. No one would find that admirable, and it certainly goes against what Jesus teaches later about giving to a needy neighbor.

But the sibling rivalry was intense thanks to their parent's favoritism. The Bible doesn't mince any words about this. Rebekah loved Jacob, and Isaac loved Esau. Both brothers were aware of this, which explains, although it doesn't excuse, their treatment of each other.

I have to backtrack just a moment here. When Rebekah, their mother, was pregnant with the twins, she had a difficult time and prayed. "LORD, if you blessed me with a child, why am I having so much trouble"? God answers her questions but then gives her some additional information. "And the younger will serve the other." So perhaps Rebekah felt somewhat justified in loving Jacob the most. But she didn't have to help God with his plan.

Years pass, and Isaac, practically blind and thinking he is dying (He isn't.), decides it's the right time to give his official blessing to Esau. Isaac wants to do this up right, make it a ceremony, so he tells Esau to kill some game and prepare a tasty dish. After they eat, Isaac will bless him. Although Esau sold his birthright, he still has a blessing coming to him.

Rebekah, eavesdropping, hears all this and concocts a scheme to have Jacob disguise himself as his brother and deceive Isaac into giving him the blessing instead. She knew this was possible because Isaac was nearly blind. Some mother, huh?

Back to our timeline. The Genesis story states their trickery works, and Isaac is indeed fooled. Some Jewish rabbis suggest that Isaac knew it was Jacob but felt Jacob deserved the blessing more than Esau anyway, even though Esau was his favorite. The foreign women Esau married brought great trouble to Isaac and Rebekah and showed Esau's disdain for his heritage and their beliefs.

Jacob lies when Isaac asks if he is Esau. Isaac gives him the blessing. Jacob and Rebekah must have worked quickly because the Bible says that Jacob had barely left when Esau showed up. He approaches Isaac with the meal, and Isaac appears confused. They both learn that they were tricked and that Isaac had already given away the blessing to Jacob. Can you imagine how Esau is feeling? Jacob took advantage of his hunger earlier, and now he has tricked him!

Esau is beside himself and pleads, "Wait, isn't there a second blessing you can give me"? Isaac says he can't do that and instead, in Genesis 27:39-40, tells Esau what the LORD told Rebekah, that he would serve his brother. Esau is furious and makes plans to kill Jacob. Rebekah, ever the eavesdropper, hears of this.

We will come back to Rebekah.

After all, the deception comes to light. As Esau is on the verge of killing his brother, Jacob, Rebekah asks Isaac to send Jacob away to her brother, Laban. She wants him to take a wife from Laban's family. (A lot of intermarrying among relatives happened back then.) But before Isaac sends him away, he blesses him again; this time, there is no question Isaac knows who he is giving a blessing to.

And wouldn't you know it, Esau is the one eavesdropping now. But Esau does the right thing (not the two wives but where they were from) this time by marrying wives from Canaan. So that's a plus for Esau.

Anyway, Jacob takes off to find Rebekah's brother, Laban. (Laban and Rebekah are cut from the same cloth as you will learn.) On this journey, Jacob spends some nights under the stars. On one such night, the LORD appears to Jacob and confirms his prior covenant with Abraham. He further states, "I am with you and will keep you wherever you go and bring you back to this land; for I will not leave you until I have done what I promised you" (Genesis 28:10-22).

I know. You are wondering why God blessed Jacob, considering what he'd done. But "God looks at the heart" (I Samuel 16:7). Jacob may have realized his sin of deceiving his father and brother by this time. It doesn't matter anyway because it's up to God how he uses man to accomplish his purpose. This night is Jacob's defining moment, but he will be detoured again, although not by his own doing. (Jacob, the deceiver, will soon learn how it feels to be the deceived.

Jacob has done an awful thing in deceiving his father and taking advantage of his brother, and yet God appears to him and gives him that promise. That should give us all hope. God can use anyone. But more will happen, and Jacob's faith will be tested. But when God gives a promise, he keeps it. And when God gives you a more, unless you throw it away forever, he will bring it to fruition.

Jacob continues his journey and is nearing his destination when he comes across a well where he meets a beautiful young woman named Rachel. He is smitten. Jacob learns that Rachel's uncle is none other than Laban, his mother's cousin, just the man he is looking for. Someone notifies Laban that a relative of his is at the well. Laban quickly goes there and insists Jacobs come home with him. Jacob is about to run into his match.

Years before, when Laban gave his sister (Rebekah) to Isaac in marriage, the Bible says that Laban noticed the ring and the bracelets given to her by Abraham's servant (Genesis: 24:30). In other words, he knew Jacob's father was wealthy. As we will learn, Laban is all about the money.

Jacob offers to work for Laban to pay for this stay. Laban insists that Jacob mustn't work for free and asks him what he thinks he should pay. Jacob says, "I will serve you several years for your daughter, Rachel." Several turn out to be seven. The Bible says it only seemed a few days to Jacob because he loved Rachel so much.

Finally, there is a wedding and a wedding night. Jacob had plenty to drink, so he didn't realize the trick played on him until the morning. He probably threw back the covers expecting to see his beautiful young wife. But her sister, Leah, is lying there instead and is not nearly as attractive. But Jacob is legally married to her now.

Crafty Laban explains that, according to tradition, fathers were obligated to marry off their oldest daughter first. In this case, Leah. He told Jacob he could marry Rachel the next week, although he would have to work *another* seven years to pay off the new debt. See what I mean about Jacob meeting his match? When I read this, I immediately thought, "What goes around comes around." If anyone deserved to be deceived, it was the deceiver himself. Every time I read this story, I have to be honest and admit a part of me says, "Jacob, you sure had that one coming."

The story continues. Within the week, Jacob and Rachel are married, and Jacob has to work for seven *more* years. Leah produces four sons for Jacob right away, while Rachel has none. Rachel is unhappy. She may be the prettier one, but Leah is the fertile one. (You did catch that Jacob was married to them both now, didn't you?)

Rachel decides to go another way and has her servant lie with Jacob so she can have a child. This practice was not uncommon back then, so hold your judgment. So begins a cycle. Rachel and Leah continue to use their servants to lie with Jacob in a kind of who-can-bear-the-most-children contest.

Leah gives birth to six sons (six of Israel's tribes) and one daughter. Rachel's servant produces one son, Dan (another of Israel's tribes). Rachel then conceives herself and gives birth to Joseph and later to Benjamin (both tribes of Israel.)

Eventually, Jacob pays off this debt and returns to his homeland. But not before he works six more years to afford to buy some sheep from crooked Laban and increase his personal wealth. Once again, Laban is unethical with Jacob. This story can be found in Genesis 30: 25-43.

I love this verse where Jacob says, "I have served your father (he's talking to Rachel) with all my strength, and yet your father has deceived me..." (Genesis 31:6-7). From one deceiver to another.

But through it all, God kept his promise to Jacob. Jacob returns home and, on that journey, encounters Esau, who he is sure will kill him. But Esau has a changed heart, runs to meet his brother, and kisses him.

If God can take a life that has been detoured for twenty years and turn it around, he can do the same for you.

Jacob had a lot of faults. He made many mistakes, but after the LORD appeared at Bethel, he acknowledged God. In Genesis 35: 3, Jacob states: "...I will make an altar to God who answered me in the day of my distress and has been with me wherever I have gone." I think those words indicate that Jacob became a changed man.

The lesson here is plain. We can screw up, but when God has a mission, he will keep reminding us of it as long as we have open ears. Unless we deliberately and intentionally throw it away, as Esau did with his inheritance, God will see our more fulfilled. But don't take a twenty-year detour if you can avoid it.

Back to Rebekah. Did she have a more? God had a calling for her because he has a calling for all of us. But there is nothing else written about Rebekah, so we don't know. Rebekah failed by deciding she knew best how God's plan (that the older son would serve the younger) should be accomplished. We have no idea how the story might have turned out if Rebekah had not jumped in and were there not a stolen birthright. God didn't need Rebekah's help. But here's the saddest part. After Jacob left to flee Esau's murderous rage, Rebekah never again saw Jacob, her favorite son.

We probably all try to help God at times. But if and when God wants our help, he will make it known. Don't be like Rebekah and take things into your own hands.

Jacob's story: Genesis 27-36, 42-50, the Old Testament

Rahab

Rahab, the prostitute. Her story is one of the most interesting detours, and the outcome of this detour filters down to an amazing climax. It's a short story.

Rahab was a prostitute in the city of Jericho in Canaan. She was a Canaanite, and the Canaanites were the enemies of Israel. Before the Israelites crossed the Jordan River, they sent spies to scout the land. (Forty years earlier, remember?) And do you remember the names of those two spies that returned with a good report? Joshua and Caleb.

Guess who is leading this battle?

Joshua! The same Joshua from forty years prior. (I certainly could have included Joshua in the Detoured More category, huh?)

The spies decide to spend the night at the house of the prostitute, Rahab. Why? Because city residents were used to seeing men going in and out of Rahab's house. Of course. Smart, huh? But somehow, the king of Jericho figures out the two spies are at her house.

When some of the king's men come to search for them, she hides them under bundles of flax on the roof. When the men ask where they are, she tells them they have already left and might still catch them if they go quickly. They run out, leaving Joshua and Caleb safe. God used Rahab to redirect the searchers and save her own family's lives, as you will read next.

She goes up to the roof to tell the spies they are safe. She is a smart woman, though. Before letting them down the wall via a rope, she makes them promise to protect her and her family when they return to fight. The two spies tell her to place a red cord out her window, signaling the Israelites not to destroy her home. She did, and she and her family were spared.

As she pleaded with the spies to spare her and her family, she affirmed her new faith in God by saying this:

".... for the LORD your God is God in heaven above and on the earth below." That was Rahab's statement of faith. Hebrews 11:31 states, "By faith, Rahab..." This was Rahab's statement of faith.

But there is so much more to her story. If you don't know this next part, you are in for a real eye-opener. Rahab's detour gets her a spot in a critical genealogy. Read Matthew 1:5-6. Rahab's name is included in the lineage of Jesus himself. It's astounding that a prostitute's name appears in Christ's genealogy, along with Abraham, David, Boaz, Ruth, and others.

Detours are not always permanent. They are not always

self-imposed. It depends on who is doing the detouring, doesn't it, and why?

What about you? Have you ever been detoured by God? Have you ever taken a self-imposed detour? How did that turn out?

Rahab's story: Joshua 2, the Old Testament. Lineage, Matthew 1: 5-6, the New Testament.

Peter

Peter was one of the original twelve disciples and one of the first chosen. He was a fisherman by trade. He believed in a coming Messiah, although it would take him some time to reconcile what he believed about the coming Messiah and what was the truth. The Jews were expecting the Messiah to be a conqueror, a liberator, and a superhero. Jesus didn't fit the bill, but I think Peter figured those attributes would show up at the right time.

Jesus WAS a conqueror but on a cross, not a throne, with love and forgiveness, and not a sword.

Peter becomes a devout follower of Jesus. He was headstrong, impulsive, and opinionated, and Jesus addressed these qualities more than once. Once again, assuming not everyone knows his story, let me recap.

Peter followed Jesus for three years and was a part of the inner circle, along with James and John. Peter is a type-A personality. Peter is the one who walked on water. Most people forget that Peter didn't *try* to walk on water; he *walked* on water. The Bible clearly states, in Matthew 14:22-33, that "Peter got out of the boat, walked on the water and came to Jesus." He didn't sink until he noticed the waves." That's more than the rest of us have done, and isn't it interesting that people remember the sinking part but not the walking part?

But he's remembered more for the worst mistake he made. And it was a big one. Not an unredeemable one, however, as we will learn. Let's get right to the betrayal.

Peter witnessed Jesus's betrayal by Judas in the Garden. He was so angry that he drew his sword and cut off the ear of one of the soldiers. Eventually, Jesus is forcibly removed from the garden and taken away for trial. Peter follows, albeit furtively. Jesus is brought into the chief priest's house.

In the outer courtyard, a fire is burning, and people are sitting around it, probably talking about what is happening. Jesus had caused quite an uproar, and politics was just as much a thing back then as it is now. Peter joins the group, perhaps thinking that Jesus will be released and set free. Or maybe he was trying to find out how much trouble he was in. Matthew 26:56 even states: "Then all the disciples left Him and fled."

Picture it. Peter has to be distraught. What is going to happen to Jesus? What about the disciples? Are they in danger? All of this might well have been going through Peter's mind. He is thinking about all this when he hears a young servant girl pointing at him and saying, "This man was also with him (meaning Jesus.)." Peter replies that she doesn't know what she's talking about; he is not a follower of Christ. A little later, another person says, "You are one of them." Again, Peter denies it, but he remains by the fire.

The Bible says another person recognizes him and calls him out about an hour later. "Certainly, this man was with him, for he too is a Galilean." Peter responds, "You don't know what you are talking about!" Peter was afraid. Afraid that if the people thought he was a follower of Jesus, he, too, would be arrested. Fear is terrible, and I'm not sure I would've handled it any better.

And while he was talking, a rooster crowed.

A verse in the book of Luke (22:61) reads, "And the LORD turned to look at Peter, and Peter remembered what he'd said at the Passover dinner." All the gospels record the event, but only Luke writes that Jesus looked straight at Peter after the rooster crowed.

Reading all four references (Luke 22:61, Matthew 26:58-75, Mark 14:53-75, and John 18:12-27, it seems there could have been an opening in the home to the courtyard, where Jesus could see Peter. Or, when Jesus was removed from that location, he might have passed by Peter. But that's just a guess. Can you imagine how Peter felt when Jesus looked straight at him? The guilt and remorse must've been overwhelming.

I haven't explained yet why the rooster crowing was a big deal in the first place. For that, you have to back up to the last supper. The disciples are eating the Passover dinner with Jesus. They have no clue what is soon to happen, even though Jesus has left hints. But the disciples didn't want to believe it. Most of us wouldn't have wanted to believe someone we love would die either.

Jesus delivers more unsettling statements, "You will all fall away...." Peter, of course, is the first to protest, maybe the only one. The Bible doesn't say. He confronts Jesus with, "Everybody else might, but I won't!!!!" (paraphrased). And then Jesus gets very specific.

*"Truly, I say unto you that this **very** night, before a rooster crows, you will deny me three times."* Once again, Peter is right there exclaiming, *"Even if I have to die with You, I will not deny you. All the disciples said the same thing."* (Matthew 26:17-35)

Picture the scene.

The disciples' words were probably tumbling out and spilling over each other, and nobody knew who was saying what. "Jesus, what are you talking about? None of us would do that! Jesus, why are you saying that? Why would you even think we would deny you?" And so on.

But Peter denied it the loudest, declaring boldly, "Even though all may fall away, yet I will not." Mark 14:31 says, "They were all saying the same thing."

Jesus has also previously stated that one of them at the table would betray him (this being different from denying). And, of course, the disciples were all over themselves, protesting they would never.

Betrayal and denial.

Judas betrayed. Peter denied. Which do you think is worse?

There was confusion earlier when Jesus dipped a morsel and gave it to Judas. But Judas knew that *Jesus* knew Judas was the betrayer (read that again) and told him, "What you do, do quickly." The disciples don't understand what this means. They assume Judas is leaving to give money to the poor or buy something for the Passover meal.

Most of the accounts of the Last Supper are relatively brief, but John 13-17 records a sermon called "The Upper Room Discourse." Interestingly, Judas never heard this because he left earlier. This is sad because Judas might have done things differently had Judas heard these sermons.

Supper is over. Things have quieted down. Jesus has quit speaking, they sing a hymn, according to Mark 26:31, and they go out to the Mount of Olives. Judas shows up, and Jesus is arrested and taken away. And then, we have the scene in the courtyard.

So, what is happening with Peter now? He is beyond belief that he denied Christ. What was going through his head? The Bible says he wept bitterly. Was he suicidal?

I have no idea what those next days were like for Peter while Jesus was being tried and beaten. I have nothing to base this on except what I understand about human nature. Still, I believe that in those three days, Peter found a way to convey to Jesus how sorry he was. I base that on the verse in Luke 24:11-12, just after the women tell the disciples that Jesus' tomb was empty.

"But these words appeared as nonsense, and they would not believe them. But Peter got up and ran to the tomb; stooping and looking in, he saw the linen wrappings only, and he went away to his home marveling at what had happened."

I believe Peter knew he was forgiven; otherwise, why be so eager to run to the grave? Had he not been forgiven, I think an empty tomb would have him shaking in his boots! Knowing we are forgiven changes how we behave. Here, Peter acts like a forgiven man to me.

Peter became one of the most influential of the original twelve apostles and helped Paul establish the New Testament church. Peter is the only apostle's name used by the angel guarding the tomb, Mark 16:7: "...but go tell the apostles and Peter that He is going ahead of you to Galilee, and you will see him there."

Peter is singled out and given his more <u>despite</u> his denial. We should be encouraged by that.

There is always hope; the story of Peter is the perfect example. During his quiet moments (if he had any), Peter must have looked back over his life and said, "Wow. How did I end up here? Who would have thought it?"

Peter is all of us at some time or another. We get sidelined by life. Things build up, and we forget our more for a while. Peter walked with his more for three years and still managed to get detoured. So, there is hope for us as well. But it is far better not to get detoured at all.

Peter's story: Matthew, Mark, Luke, John, Acts, 1 & 2 Peter in the New Testament.

NINE: THRUST-UPON MORES

What is a trust-upon more? I would call it an unexpected more, but thrust-upon seemed a bit more dramatic, and these examples are certainly that. They could also be called turned-around mores because, undoubtedly, lives were turned around in each of these examples. As followers of Christ, we all live turned-around lives in some way or another, don't we?

A thrust-upon-more is a more we didn't see coming.

Paul

I love a good turnaround story, don't you? It was hard to decide where to put the following example.

We read all the time about people who've started from nothing and risen to greatness, and we are encouraged and inspired. Who doesn't like those kinds of stories?

I have a real-life example from my own extended family. I have two twin nephews who come from a very broken home. Their grandmother raised them, and while she did her best, she fell short. One ended up in jail for a short period.

Now, they both have very successful corporate jobs with McDonald's, yes, the burger chain. I am so glad we got to be a small part of their lives, and I have no doubt my husband's example and acceptance of them made a big difference.

But the best turnaround story is found in Scripture. There is not another story to equal it. It's the story of the apostle Paul.

Depending on the timeline, Paul could be a 'detoured' more, a right more, or a wrong more. I chose to place him here because this is such a dramatic story, and more was definitely thrust upon him. It's the story of a man who persecuted Christians for years but became a believer and the leader of the new faith movement known as the Way. I wasn't going to include the details because I assume that because I know them, everyone else does, too. However, the one thing you learn from writing a book is never to assume anything.

In my first book, *Depression Has a Big Voice,* I have a chapter titled "Distraction Is a Good Thing." The concept was so apparent to me. I assumed everyone knew how distraction works and why, and I almost didn't include it in the book. As it turned out, that's one of the chapters still eliciting the most positive comments.

The story of Paul begins with the story of Stephen, the apostle chosen to replace Judas, in Acts chapter seven. The disciples appointed Stephen after Pentecost to distribute food and aid to the poorer members of the early church. (Acts 6:1-7) Stephen is further described as a man "full of faith and the holy spirit."

One day, in response to a rebel group seeking to defame the disciples' teachings, Stephen delivers a scorching sermon in verses Acts 7:1- 53. These verses are an excellent recap of the history of the Jewish people and how God dealt with them through the ages. It's worth the read.

Those in the audience were furious. The Bible says in Acts 8:2

that they were cut to the quick and began gnashing their teeth at him. The truth hurts. They were mad! So mad they drove him out of the city and stoned him to death.

But before that, the witnesses took off their coats and laid them at the feet of a young man named Saul. (This is like when you go to a wedding reception, and one person is designated to watch the women's purses so they can dance. Except this is a stoning.) Anyway, Saul, the keeper of the coats, watches while the other men stone Steven to death. This is Saul's first introduction in the Bible. Not too stellar.

Acts 8:1 states, "Saul was in hardy agreement with them." In other words, he was cheering them on. That day ignited great persecution against the early church, and guess who was now an active participant? Saul. Verse 3 states that Saul "ravaged" the church by going from home to home, "dragging off men and women," and imprisoning them. The word "ravage" means "ravaging like a wild beast" and shows Saul's hatred for Jesus' followers.

It's safe to assume that dragging them off meant beating them into submission first. And it doesn't mention what happened to any children that might have been in the home. Were they left to fend for themselves? And what about the elderly or disabled? Were they thrown in prison, too? We don't know these answers. But we can surmise a couple of things.

First of all, Saul was one violent, mean, hateful man. Picture it for yourself. What do you imagine? I imagine violent scenes, people screaming and fighting back, and Paul striking them severely. I imagine bloodied bodies and terrified people screaming and trying to get away. All this is to paint a very dark picture of Saul, precisely what Luke, the author of Acts, intends. He is setting the stage for what happens after Saul's conversion. He wants us to see the vivid contrast.

A little background on Saul before we get to the big scene. Saul was a wealthy, well-educated Jew. As such, he adhered to all the teachings of the Torah and knew them well. He could probably quote every one of the 613 laws of the Torah. Now, to the good part, Acts 9:1-18.

"Now Saul, still breathing threats and murder against the disciples of the LORD, went to the high priest and asked for letters from him to the synagogues at Damascus so that if he found any belonging to the Way, both men and women, he might bring them back to Jerusalem."

As he was traveling and approaching Damascus, a light from heaven suddenly flashed around him. It was so intense he fell to the ground. Paul was scared. Cowering in the dirt, he heard a voice saying, *'Saul, Saul, why are you persecuting me?*

And he said, *"Who are you, LORD?"* And he said, *"I am Jesus whom you are persecuting, but get up and enter the city and it will be told you what you must do."*

Paul is dumbstruck. He hasn't persecuted Jesus. Besides, the man is dead. Or is he?

This experience begins the start of one of the biggest thrust-upon-mores in history. God is going to take Saul and change him completely. He will only be a whisper of the man he used to be. And why is that? It's because Saul will receive a call that directly contradicts the life he led up to this point. As he writes later, *"becomes a new man, the old is passed away and all things become new."*

Paul penned those words in 2 Corinthians 5:17. When you consider his past, the words take on new meaning now, don't they? He knew from his own experience what he was talking about. It's like when I write about depression. What I write carries some weight because I've been there. Same with Paul. He was there and knew what it felt like to become a new person. He speaks with authenticity.

But there is more. Paul has been struck blind for three days. Can you imagine? Hearing such a message from Christ himself and then becoming blind? He had been spiritually blind; now, he is physically blind. But his sight gets restored, and he becomes a "light to the Gentiles."

Saul is called Paul throughout the rest of the Bible. The names could have been interchangeable anyway, like John or Jack Kennedy, but wouldn't you want to change your name if you had had Saul's reputation?

It's interesting to read how the disciples struggle to receive this once fierce adversary into their midst. Still, they do, and Paul becomes the greatest missionary in the Bible. Paul wrote thirteen books in the New Testament, which is almost half of the twenty-seven books total. Some of our most beloved scripture passages were written by the hand of this former persecutor of Christians.

What does this all mean?

It means that God can turn around anyone and give them a more. But Paul's story can be anyone's story. It's probably in the Bible for that reason. It illustrates how God can use and gift any of us with more. It's never too late. Our history is never too damaged; our lives are never too unredeemable. The story of Paul demonstrates this.

Paul's history is extensive. His books give some of the best explanations of our standing and salvation in Christ. He is considered the greatest missionary of all time, the G.O.A.T (greatest of all times). Paul's life stands alone in the Bible for its impact on Christianity and the church.

Paul's story: Acts, Romans, 1 & 2 Corinthians, Galatians, Ephesians, Philippians, Colossians, 1 & 2 Thessalonians, Timothy, Titus, Philemon, the New Testament.

Esther

The Book of Esther and the Book of Ruth are the only two books of the Bible named after women. While their stories differ, both stories reveal powerful and heroic young women. I love the book of Esther, but primarily because of Haman, whose story you have already read. But Esther is the heroine, hands down.

Her story begins. Esther is a beautiful young woman. There is a local beauty pageant, and the winner will replace Queen Vashti, who was dethroned because she refused to be ogled during one of the king's drunken brawls.

Esther is taken into the king's palace and given royal beauty treatments along with all the other virgins. Esther's beauty makes her a standout, and one of the king's overseers singles her out for special treatment, a twelve-month spa. The king's staff greatly admired Esther as she didn't ask for anything special during that time.

She wins the beauty pageant, and the king even falls in love with her. Because of the evil Haman, a plan is underfoot to kill all the Jews. The king doesn't know that Esther is a Jew, as her uncle, Mordecai, instructed her to keep that secret for now. But when the Jews are threatened with annihilation, Mordecai says she must now make her ancestry known. He speaks those famous words to her, "....and who knows whether you have not attained royalty *for such a time as this*?" We all have a "for such a time as this," and our more may very well be for such a time as well.

God's more is always well-timed. It's unique to us and our story. His more always comes right when it should, but we must be active participants, which is precisely what happens next.

Esther takes the reins. She hears what her uncle suggests but comes up with her own plan. Instead of rushing in to tell the king, she asks for prayer and fasting for three days while she thinks through her plans. Esther is a book filled with intrigue and reads like a mystery novel, except the author is God.

Esther plans banquets for the king and invites Israel's archenemy, Haman. She manipulates the banquets, so Haman is led like a pig to the slaughter. Too late, Haman learns what Queen Esther has done. He ends up hanging on the gallows he built for Esther's uncle Mordecai. (The details are in the story of Haman.)

Esther puts her uncle in charge of Haman's former house. Esther falls at the king's feet and begs him to stop the slaughter of the Jews. He can't because he made the decree irrevocable. But the king does come up with a plan.

He allows the Jews to defend themselves and gives them about eight months to prepare. The battle begins, and in this first round, the Jews kill five hundred people of their enemy. The king asks Esther what else he can do for her. She asks that Haman's ten sons be hanged. They are. (I'll bet that surprised you.) In all, the Jews killed 75,000 of those who hated them but did not take any plunder.

Esther stands head and shoulders above so many. I love that once Mordecai made the plight of the Jews known to her, she paused and considered what to do. She didn't rush ahead foolishly.

Sometimes, our more requires sitting back for some time to think. And when we do, our more begins to take shape. Remember, our more doesn't usually just fall in our laps, all gift-wrapped and ready to go.

Esther's story: Book of Esther in the Old Testament.

Job

Job never asked for his more, and what he went through to find it was terrible.

One day, the sons of God came to present themselves to God, and Satan was among them. Think of it like this. These sons of God are angels returning from wandering the earth on assignment. They are coming at God's request to give an accounting of what they've done and observed. (Barnes' Notes on the Bible.) While Satan's presence has not been requested, he shows up anyway. He is still an angel, too, albeit a fallen one.

God asks Satan: "Where did you come from?" Satan replies he'd been wandering the earth. God asks, "Did you see my servant, Job? There is no one like him on earth. He is blameless and reveres me."

Satan counters with, "Well, why wouldn't he? He has everything he needs or wants and is living well. But would he be so blameless if he lost it all? Would he honor you then?" (Let me tell you, I hope I'm never singled out like this.)

God takes the challenge and tells Satan he is, more or less, handing Job over to him because he's sure Job won't cave. "But you can't hurt Job himself," God says.

We don't know how close to this conversation these following events occur, but in fast succession, Job receives a string of terrible news. The first messenger tells Job that his livestock and those tending them have been destroyed. It gets worse.

Before that messenger has quit talking, another messenger tells him that all his servants and sheep have been burned to death. But yet *another* messenger who speaks over the other two tells Job the worst of the bad news.

A great wind had blown apart his eldest son's house, where all his sons and daughters were gathered together having dinner. They have all been killed.

Don't shoot the messenger.

Job's grief overcomes him, yet he falls to the ground and worships God. Scripture states in Job 1:22, "Through all this Job did not sin or blame God."

I am not Job.

For a second time, the sons of God approach God, and Satan has, once again, snuck in with them. God brings up Job and tells Satan that his plan didn't work. Job is still without fault, and Job still loves God. Satan is now ready to drive the final nail.

"Yes, but what if I touch Job himself, his body, and make him so ill he wants to die? Let's see what happens then."

Once again, God permits Satan to make Job ill somehow, but he is forbidden to kill him. What does Satan do? He inflicts Job with excruciatingly painful boils from the top of his head to the bottom of his feet. Job 2:10 states he has four friends who come to sit with him during this horrible period of his life. Sitting with someone during their grief is always the best approach, but these friends couldn't leave it there. Through lengthy discussions, they tell Job all this is happening to him because of some sins Job committed. They keep telling Job to repent.

Job and three friends go back and forth in conversation, the friends telling him he has sinned and Job saying he hasn't. A fourth friend, who has remained silent because he is much younger, now speaks.

He is angry with the other friends because they have not proven their case against Job. At the same time, he is upset with Job for trying to justify himself before God and asking God to explain himself. He also suggests Job has sinned and needs to own up to it, but his words are closer to the truth.

Job maintains his innocence, but he is also somewhat proud. We should never take pride in our obedience and righteous living, but like Job, we should not take guilt that isn't ours either. God soon addresses the issue with Job: Job wanted answers for his suffering. Job felt he was owed them after all he had been through. God is about to show up and remind Job who he's talking to, the Creator of the universe.

God begins asking many rhetorical questions, like, "Have you ever in your life commanded the morning and caused the dawn to know its place?" Chapters 38-41 are some of the most beautiful chapters in the Bible.

Job hears every question and realizes he is wrong to criticize God for his dealings with him. He was wrong for asking for explanations. (Anyone listening?) As God paints a picture of creation to show his superiority, Job is humbled and repents. God is very angry with Job's friends because they have not accurately reflected who God is and what part he played in Job's sufferings.

He reminds them Job had remained righteous and never turned his back on God through it all. His problem was that he wanted answers. Don't we all? The fourth friend, Elihu, escapes God's wrath because he has spoken some truth.

The three friends were told to offer a burnt offering for themselves *and* Job so that God would not deal with them according to their mistakes. And then something interesting happens. Job shows what a righteous man he is by praying for his friends. After Job prays, it is *then* that God restores everything to Job twofold except for his children, which he restores in the same number. I find the timing of these events very interesting. It was after Job prayed for his friends that God restored everything.

If you're hearing this story for the first time, you must wonder,

"Why would God allow all that to happen to a truly righteous man?" And I'm afraid I can't answer that. This question, "Why do good men suffer?" is the existential question we all face. Scholars and theologians throughout history have tried to answer this question. I won't even try. I will say that God's ways *are* hard to understand at times. There's nothing wrong with admitting that. Besides, God knows we all have those questions tucked away in the back of our minds, whether we voice them or not.

But what is Job's more? We could say he ended up with more than he started with, but I don't think that would be accurate because all of his children died, and I doubt increased wealth made up for that. I believe Job's more is found in Job 42:5, where Job states, "I had heard reports about you, but now my eyes have seen you."

Up to this point, Job's knowledge of God was based on what he had been taught and his own assumptions. Now, Job has heard God's words spoken from God's mouth and is confronted with the living God. Job's spiritual eyes are opened. He admits that he doesn't need answers. God's presence is answer enough.

Read Job's response in Job 42:1-6. They are words we need to memorize, especially these words from verse 2, *"I know you can do all things, and no purpose of yours can be thwarted."* No God-given more can be thwarted, either.

Job's more was renewed and refreshed based on his intimate experience with the living God. His faith became more, and he learned God could be trusted.

Job's story: Book of Job in Old Testament.

Mary-mother of Jesus

Could there be any better example of a thrust-upon more than the story of Mary, the virgin mother of Jesus, being told she would bear a child without having sexual relations with a man? When we think of Mary, we go immediately to the visit with the angel and then to the foot of the cross. We seldom think of the events leading up to that or all the events in between.

Mary was a very young Jewish girl about whom we know very little. The New Testament does not state her birth, death, appearance, or age. The virgin birth is only recorded in Matthew and Luke.

She is mentioned explicitly at only a few events in Jesus's adult life. She is vital in scripture, yet we know little about her. But maybe being the mother of Jesus might be enough!

Based on Proverbs 31, we have a general idea about a woman's life in Biblical times. Many women made and sold garments for a profit; they were retailers. They cooked, taught their children, managed the affairs of their families, bought and sold properties, and much more. One wonders what the men did!

While Mary wouldn't have done some of those things as she was too young, she knew they were in her future. We can assume that Mary was modest and hard-working as she did not come from a wealthy family. God knew Mary would face much in her life, so he chose someone up for the job.

Luke 1:28 says the angel visited Mary in the sixth month of Elizabeth's (Mary's cousin) pregnancy. "And coming in, he said to Mary, "Greetings, favored one. The LORD is with you". I want to stop right here. I've lost count of the times I've read this verse but never noticed something.

This angel appeared human. He *walked* into her home. The scripture doesn't say he appeared in a mist, a cloud, or with wings batting. It's almost like he's the next-door neighbor because you notice Mary is not the least bit unnerved that a stranger has walked into her house. It's like she's used to people coming into her home unannounced.

However, Mary does wonder why he addresses her the way he does, "favored one," but she is not shocked he is standing there. He's someone who's come to visit. But then, the angel tells her why he is there, and things change. Mary questions the validity of what he tells her. But when the angel tells her about her cousin Elizabeth, how could a stranger know that?

At this point, Mary must realize this is an angel. She responds, "May it be to me as you have said." The angel leaves, and in verse thirty-nine, the Bible says Mary *hurried* out to the hill country to visit her cousin. The two cousins were close because we don't hurry to see someone we don't like, right?

Elizabeth sees Mary coming and knows without asking what has happened and proclaims Mary to be the mother of the long-awaited Messiah. I suggest this is when Mary finally grasps what the angel told her. Sometimes, God uses another person to reinforce his call on our lives. At this point, she is ecstatic with the news and bursts forth to utter the famous words we know at the Magnificat.

She could have spoken those words before visiting her cousin, but she didn't. I believe it was Elizabeth's proclamation when Mary fully realized and embraced her more. And what a more it was. There would never be another one like it for all of eternity.

Mary matured during the next three months as she stayed with her cousin. Like Paul, who spent three years in Arabia alone with God after Jesus appeared to him, Mary also needed time to process her revelation. This is common. Stepping back to process a call God has made in your life is a good idea.

I can only imagine what she thought about in those three months. How much did she understand? I wonder what she felt as she watched her son grow and saw the danger that always seemed to surround him. She knew Jesus to be a great teacher, but how much did she know about his death and resurrection? She was at the crucifixion, saw the empty tomb, and was in the upper room with the disciples after the resurrection. (Acts 1:13-14)

There is no scripture to support that Mary knew how Jesus would die. Nobody knew. Not even the disciples. Jesus told them in so many words, but they didn't take those words literally. Mary must have heard Jesus speak about eternity, but did she ever imagine the scene? She was the only person present for both his birth and his death, Joseph having apparently died.

Could she have told the angel, "No, not doing this?" And if she had, would he have found someone else? Who knows?

But perhaps I should have picked Joseph as my example, as he is the unsung hero in this story. Many people think only Mary descended from the Davidic line. She did, but so did Joesph.

Joseph descended from David through Solomon, and that was the chosen line of David for someone to be considered king. Hence, Jesus was the son of David by *biological* descent through Mary and the king of Israel by *legal* right through Joseph. Scripture was fulfilled that Jesus would be born from the house of David. That was from Joseph's line, not Mary's.

He chose Joseph just like he did Mary. We sometimes forget that Mary and Joseph both received visits from the angel Gabriel. I guess you could say this was a marriage made in heaven.

Do we even have to ask what was Mary's more? I think not.

Mary and Joesph's story: Luke 1 & 2, the New Testament.

TEN: BACKBURNER MORES

Let's look at those who put their mores on the backburners through neglect and wrong turns. Some never retrieved it.

We lose our more when we are careless with it. Isn't that how we lose anything? We put it on a shelf, in a drawer, or, if you're anything like me, in a safe place you soon forget. There it stays, collecting dust.

Moses

Moses is a back-burner more if there ever was one. I will speed right by his early history except to tell you this. Because of a degree by Pharoah that all Jewish babies were to be killed, Moses's mother put him in a little papyrus basket, placing it in the Nile River. The Bible says she couldn't hide him any longer. His older sister, Miriam, decides to watch and see what happens to her little brother. Whether her mother told her to do this or she did it on her own, we don't know.

We know that Pharoah's daughter was bathing in the river nearby. She spots the basket with the three-month-old in it and feels pity for the child. (Exodus 2:6). Miriam approaches Pharoah's daughter and asks if she wants her to find a nursemaid for the child. Miriam hurries, gets her mother, Yocheved, and brings her back. Her mother is hired to be her child's nursemaid until he is weaned. When Moses was about three, Pharaoh's daughter took on the role of mother. She named him Moses, which means "one who draws out."

When Moses was about forty, he witnessed an Egyptian beating a Hebrew. Moses killed the man after first making sure (he thought anyway) that no one was watching. The next day, Moses interrupted a fight between two Hebrew men and tried to break it up. In that altercation, the men let Moses know he had no right to speak because they saw what he did the day before. So much for Moses, thinking no one saw him.

This news scared Moses because he figured everyone knew about it, and sure enough, someone did. Pharaoh called for his assassination, and Moses hightailed it out of Egypt, where he became a shepherd *for forty years.* Moses had cast his lot with his people but wasn't ready yet to lead them.

Forty years later, God decided it was time for Moses to receive his more. God speaks to Moses through the famous burning bush incident and gives him an enormous more, rescue the millions of enslaved Jews, and takes them to a land flowing with milk and honey. (Exodus 4: 3 & 4.)

Moses, like many of us, resisted his more. Who can blame him? He argues why he can't do what God has just told him to do. When you think about it, how brave (or foolish) was Moses to say no to God, who just appeared in a burning bush that never burnt up? I wouldn't have known what to say, and although I was a state champion debater in high school and still love a good back and forth I would have been speechless.

Moses' arguments don't work, but God allows Aaron, his natural brother, to speak for him when they meet with the Pharoah. According to a midrash (Rabbinic biblical interpretation), Aaron initiates the first three plagues.

A careful reading of Exodus will show several times when God talks with both Moses and Aaron. How long Aaron was the mouthpiece, I don't know. From reading the first sixteen chapters, it appears Aaron was Moses's spokesperson until God explained how he would provide quails and manna for the Israelites. Then, Moses began speaking on his own. (Exodus 8:9).

We can find our more, but it might take some time before it becomes fully functional. God set Moses aside for forty years to prepare Moses for his upcoming more. Moses learned leadership while tending sheep, a lonely occupation that gives one much time to think and reflect.

After bringing the last Israelites across the river, I like to think that Moses danced a happy dance. and raised his fist towards heaven and said, "LORD, we did it!" I know I did after I wrote my first book. As my son said, seeing his mother's name on a book cover was surreal. It was to me, too.

Moses's story: Exodus 2 - Deuteronomy 34:5, in the Old Testament.

Joshua

Joshua is one of my favorite heroes in the Old Testament. He is first brought to our attention as one of twelve spies sent out to scope out Canaan. He is number five on the list, as found in Numbers 13:8. But if you look at that list, you won't see "Joshua," but you will see "Hoshea." Moses changed his name (although the name Joshua is used before this, as recorded in verse 16. The mention here has more to do with getting the historical record correct. Hoshea means "salvation." Joshua means, "YAHWEH is salvation." I read many commentaries, and most seem to agree that Hoshea's name change to Joshua is because he was destined to be the temporal savior of his people. That seems fitting.

As long as Moses lives, Joshua is learning and growing into his name. Moses realizes he is dying and declares to the Israelites that he will not cross the Jordan. Moses states, "Joshua is the one who will cross over to the Jordan. Joshua found his more after serving Moses faithfully for many years.

My favorite story is in Joshua, chapter four, when the Israelites are getting ready to cross the Jordan River into Canaan. But before they do, Joshua tells the heads of each tribe to stop in the middle and for each of them to carry out a stone. They must have been good-sized because he tells them to carry the stones on their shoulders. Those stones would remind them of all God has done for the nation. One word, "remember," says it all.

I have a small red ceramic bowl in my bathroom filled with stones. On those stones, I wrote the word "Remember," and on the back, I wrote the scripture reference, Joshua 4:5-7. Joshua is the one who finally leads the Israelites to the promised land after winning the battle of Jericho. The sun even stood still for him.

One of the most quoted verses from Joshua is Joshua 8:25: "Do not be afraid; do not be discouraged. Be strong and courageous..." These words are spoken by a man who found his more after serving in the shadow of a great leader for forty years.

Again, we should be encouraged. Our mores may take some time to come to fruition, but the process is as exciting as the outcome.

Joshua's story: 31:23, Numbers 11:28, 27:18, book of Joshua in Old Testament.

King Saul

Some people in Scripture lost their more due to pride and jealousy. King Saul was such an example. He was tall, dark, and handsome. The Israelite nation wanted a king, and God delivered one, despite the prophet Samuel telling them a king wasn't a good idea.

Saul was appointed the first king of Israel, which should have been enough for him. And it was for a time. Somewhere along the way, Saul took his eyes off his more. He put his more on the shelf, forgot where he put it, and because of that, committed some serious wrongs (I Samuel 13 and 15). God ended up taking it away from him.

A young Shepherd boy comes to his attention, and that same young boy ends up killing the giant, Goliath, who has been tormenting the people. Saul brings David into his court. But Saul ends up hating David because David began receiving all the accolades that Saul felt should have been his. Jealousy becomes his downfall, just like with Haman. Things might have been different if Saul had just remembered where he'd put his more. But by now, it was lost, and so was he.

He made it his life's mission to kill David, only to be killed himself. Let me ask you a question. Have you ever been excited about a vision you've had? (No, not that kind.) You sense God leading you in a specific direction. You pursue it for a few months, but sooner or later, the desire fades away, and you almost forget having it in the first place. When you are alone with your thoughts, you sadly remember that time, that vision you once had. Where did it go, you wonder? What happened?

You lost the vision because you didn't give it the proper attention. You put your vision on the shelf, and like King Saul, you forgot about it. Now, it feels lost.

Many people have recognized their purpose, passion, or call but never pursued it because they tucked it away somewhere until the right time, but that time never came. So, they leave it on the shelf to gather dust. It has become a memory of what might have been.

We are likely to lose our more when we neglect it. It's that way in marriages and relationships. If we neglect our friendships, we will lose them. If we neglect our job, we will get fired. If we neglect our health, we might end up in the hospital. If we neglect our more long enough, it might get lost. Should we ever find it again, it might require a lot more work to develop it once again. But God can always turn things around, as we have learned. He is the God of turnarounds.

Your more might not look the same again. You might have to rev up some passion about it because your excitement has waned. It will need to be rekindled. It can still get accomplished because, with God, nothing is impossible, but it will be more challenging.

When God reveals something to you, consider it a precious jewel. Do you put a precious jewel on the shelf and forget about it? No. You look at it often. You dust it off. You turn it around in your hands, examining it from different angles. A pastor once told me years ago, "Don't doubt in the dark what God has revealed in the light." I've never forgotten that. And when I'm writing, I feel like I'm getting nowhere and thinking, "What am I doing? I think of what my pastor told me.

Keep your more where you can see it.

Saul's story: I Samuel 9:1, 2, and 31-44 in Old Testament.

John Mark

Next, we look at John Mark. This is the same John Mark who wrote the book of Mark in the Bible, so I will refer to him as Mark. By the way, the book of Mark is the oldest in the New Testament.

Some people would say we shouldn't make assumptions when studying the men and women of the Bible. The conflict between Mark and Paul has always fascinated me, and I've never fully embraced the popular conclusion. But let me ask you. When you think of persons and stories in Scripture, don't you let your imagination wander a little? I hope you do because it's a great way to "live" the stories.

But let's move on to Mark. No one knows why Mark left Paul and Barnabas on Paul's missionary journey. The Bible does not clarify it. So, my assumptions, because I have done my homework, are also worth considering.

Mark and Barnabas were cousins. Barnabas and Saul grew very close, as Barnabas was the one who persuaded the twelve disciples to let Paul come on board. That the disciples needed persuading is obvious; as we've learned from Paul's story, he had been a vicious persecutor of Christians before his conversion. Many feared them still and doubted that this new man, now called Paul, was sincere. The disciples might have thought he could have been what we call today a "mole."

Mark accompanied Paul and Barnabas on their first missionary journey. They were on the island of Cyprus when John left in the middle of the trip. He returned home to Jerusalem. Scripture does not say why. Barnabas suggested his cousin accompany them again when the second missionary journey was planned. Paul said no, not after deserting them the first time Acts 15:36-41). Paul and Barnabas have a sharp disagreement.

We know that before his conversion, Paul was vicious in how he dragged people out of their homes to take them to jail. I picture an angry, vindictive man because that is what scripture says. Remember, Paul even watched Stephen, the first martyr, die and held the coats of those doing the stoning! After Paul's conversion, we know he changed. There is no question he became a new person in Christ. His whole life turned around. But as our personalities are primarily ingrained, I will suggest that there was still an "edge" to Paul. I use Galatians 5:12 as an indication. *"I wish that those who trouble you would even mutilate themselves."* That's someone with an edge if ever I heard one, wouldn't you say?

Mark had been a follower of Jesus. He *knew* Jesus; he listened to Jesus. For three years, Mark was learning from Christ. Mark had the proper credentials, so it's easy to see why Barnabas would suggest him as a likely addition to Paul's first missionary journey.

But it's not hard to imagine the issues between the two. Paul was a relative newcomer to the faith, and Mark had followed Jesus for three years. Mark abruptly left Paul right in the middle of that trip, whatever the issue. Did they argue about something? Like Paul bringing the message to the Gentiles?

Could there have been a family emergency?

Was it a personality conflict? That very well could have been it. Not everybody gets along, and not everybody has to. The Bible only says we are to love one another, but it never suggests everyone will get along with everyone else. Even the original twelve had their issues. Isn't it great that Scripture doesn't sugarcoat these kinds of problems? It makes the men and women of the Bible so much more relatable to us.

An interesting side note. Paul and Mark weren't that far apart in age. Paul was a young man in Acts; we know the disciples were very young. Some scholars suggest they were all teenagers, with the youngest only thirteen. Others suggest slightly older. That Paul and Mark were close in age could also be why they were at odds with each other. That's a lot of testosterone. Also, in Acts 13:5, the Bible states John was with them as a *helper*. John might have thought, a *helper*? Excuse me, didn't I follow Jesus for three years, and I'm a *helper*? What's up with that?

These young men were just beginning their first journey and had to get used to working with each other. The three left the island as they had "missioned" around it and were ready to move on, so they "put out to sea" and arrived at Perga, where John left and returned to Jerusalem.

Some authors say Mark was a momma's boy, but nowhere does the Bible say that. His mother was wealthy. Mark left Paul and Barnabas right in the middle of the journey, which suggests there was a misunderstanding of some sort. However, we know

Paul felt Mark had abandoned them because of the disagreement that occurred when Barnabas suggested they bring him along on another journey. Paul is still apparently upset about Mark's abrupt departure. If he had a right to be, we can only surmise.

Maybe Mark needed time to think through things. Perhaps he genuinely felt a call from God to leave. Acts 13: 2-3 states that the Holy Spirit set apart Paul and Barnabas, and the church leaders commissioned them by laying on of hands. Mark wasn't. He wasn't even there. Therefore, Mark may not have felt the same intensity for the mission. Maybe he never should have gone in the first place. Perhaps he realized this was not his more.

Later, in Colossians, where Paul is a prisoner, Mark is with Paul again as Paul ends the letter indicating John is with him. They must have patched things up by this time. Mark also accompanies Barnabas on the second mission trip. Near the end of his life, Paul writes, *"Only Luke is with me. Pick up Mark and bring him with you, for he is useful to me for service."* Whatever the issue was, they worked around it.

We know Mark found his more because he wrote the gospel of Mark. He walked with Jesus and listened to his teachings. He witnessed his transfiguration. In my opinion, this is not the type of person who just left a mission for no good reason.

Mark, by this time, had found his more again. What could have been the end of ministry was now just the beginning.

Mark wrote the first and most action-packed account of his

time with Jesus

There are times when we all, for whatever reason, find ourselves at a crossroads. Should we continue or not? Is it really our more? We end up basing our opinions on our emotions, which is always risky business. Or on personalities, even riskier. Or, worst of all, what other people think.

I think we all misplace our mores now and then. After all, it's pretty hard to stay purpose-focused all the time. Life has its demands over which we have little control. Things happen, right? We have to deal with them right away. We don't have a choice, at least not for the time being. Intentionally putting our more on hold differs significantly from just letting it happen.

Say to yourself, "OK, I need to concentrate elsewhere right now. I'm putting it on hold, but not forever." When we make a conscious decision like this, we recognize it's temporary. We acknowledge that other people or situations demand our attention, but we are not giving up. That's very different from just letting your more slide due to lack of inattention for no good reason. That's how mores die.

If you've had to waylay your purpose for a good reason, look at it again when you can. Keep looking at it from different angles. Keep considering it. Maybe you can repurpose your more for now until you can tackle the whole thing head-on again.

Mark put his more on the back burner for a time but ended up writing the beautiful words we know as the gospel of John.

ELEVEN: THROWN AWAY MORES

I wished this wasn't even a chapter I would have to write. This kind of more is the saddest. The following examples focus on those who've lost their more and those who never found his. We have to start with the dawn of time for the most famous and far-reaching thrown- away more than the story of Adam and Eve. Where to begin?

But remember, if you are wondering if you've thrown away yours, it's not too late. God still has a purpose and plan for you. These examples below all had ample opportunity to turn around and make changes. They had ample opportunity to pursue their more.

But they didn't.

Adam and Eve

Think about this. Adam and Eve lived in a perfect world, extravagant and limitless. Looking to their future, they saw only more, upon more, upon more. Adam and Eve walked with God. Let me repeat. They walked with God daily, having intimate conversations with Him. It was a perfect world. God only placed a few commandments on them.

1. Be fruitful and multiply.

2. Fill the earth and master it.

3. Restrict their diet to fruit and veggies.

4. Don't eat from the Tree of the Knowledge of Good and Evil.

But they exercised their free will as well. The Bible doesn't use the words free will, but every time we make a choice, that's free will: we exert our will freely. The ability to choose is because we have free will, and good and bad options are abundant in every chapter of the Bible.

More must've gotten to be too much for Adam and Eve. How is that even possible? But the serpent promised them *even more* if Eve would eat from the tree of good and evil. He told them they would become like God, knowing good and evil. Their knowledge would equal His, and they would be like God. They wanted more on top of the more they already had and not for any altruistic reasons. They were indulgent and selfish. This more was not from God.

Adam and Eve were forewarned, too. God himself told them they were not to eat from that tree, every other tree, but that one.

I don't get how they would even know what evil was and why they would want to. It's an oddity of the creation story I don't quite get, but no one else does either. We all know what happened. Satan convinces Eve that she will not die if she eats the fruit. She believes him and eats the fruit, gives some to Adam, and he eats as well. They are now aware of their nakedness and, for the first time, feel something new, embarrassment. They cover themselves with whatever. They don't die immediately, so they may have thought they got away with it.

God looks for them one evening and asks, "Where are you?" Of course, God knew their exact location. This occasion might well have been their one chance at redemption. Here was their opportunity to apologize and ask God's forgiveness, although forgiveness wasn't even a thing then. So maybe just admitting what they had done would've been enough.

But, no, like way too many people, they cast blame elsewhere, Adam blaming Eve and Eve blaming the serpent. Talk about marital disharmony. God delivers punishment. Eve will experience pain in childbirth, and her husband will rule over her. Adam will toil to make a living.

They are kicked out of their perfect world, their perfect more. They would now experience mortality and a host of other human struggles. Don't you wonder if they looked at each other and cried pitifully, "What were we thinking?" There more was selfish and self-edifying, and they and the rest of humanity paid an enormous price.

Not too far removed from them, we have another example of a throwaway more.

Their story: Genesis 1-4 in the Old Testament.

Esau

As you recall, they were twin brothers who were each favored by one parent over the other. Jacob's story has been told. This is Esau's.

Esau's story requires little explanation because it's so obvious. We know Esau had been out hunting. According to scripture, when he came in, he was famished; "about to die" is how the NASB describes it. He asks his younger brother for some of the stew he sees bubbling on the stove. Jacob, as you read earlier, makes a deal with his brother. He wants to buy Esau's birthright for a bowl of stew.

Esau's claim he was about to die of starvation is not valid. We've all heard people say that. But Esau wasn't about to die of hunger. He could've killed an animal if needed. Maybe he forgot to pack a lunch. More worried about his stomach than his soul, Esau agrees immediately to sell his birthright and makes an oath to seal the deal. There is no sign he thought for two seconds about it. He threw away his more just that quickly.

Of course, he later misses out on his blessing because Jacob and his conniving mother devise a devious plan to fool Isaac. When they do, Esau loses out once again. But he hated Jacob way before that happened. Genesis 25:34, "Esau ate and drank, and rose and went on his way. Thus, Esau despised his brother."

Interestingly, he hated Jacob even though Jacob gave him what he wanted! Can you imagine how much more he hated him after losing out on the blessing as well.? We know he did because later in Genesis (27:41), Esau vows to kill him. ".... my father is going to die soon; then I will kill my brother Jacob."

Esau has already shown he wasn't interested in spiritual things by marrying two women from a heathen nation who worshipped idols. These women brought grief to both Isaac and Rebekah.

I believe Esau probably did regret selling his birthright, though. Do you know how sometimes you regret something and are so mad at yourself that you act inappropriately? Children do it all the time. Hate often rides on the coattails of guilt. After overhearing the instruction to Jacob not to marry someone from a heathen county, his subsequent third marriage was to a woman from Ishmael's line.

Who knows what God might have accomplished with Esau? But when we disregard the holy and put our appetites, whatever form they take, above our more, we might also throw away our more. When Esau threw away his birthright, he admitted spiritual blessings weren't all that important to him. The faith of his father, Isaac, meant nothing to him, which meant God didn't either.

Our more can be staring us right in the face, but our immediate desires overshadow it, and we throw it away. Esau's greed overshadowed his birthright and his blessing.

Esau's story: Genesis 26:34 through 27:42 and Genesis 32: 1-33:20, in the Old Testament.

Solomon

Here was a man who had it all.

According to a book by Rabbi Joseph Telushkin, Solomon was David's favorite son. I wonder if that's because Solomon was the son conceived by Bathsheba. He was to be David's successor. However, another son named Adonijah grabbed the throne before Solomon was declared king. It was like a coup. David is old at the time and knows nothing about this until Bathsheba tells him what has happened and reminds David that he promised her that Solomon, their son, would be his successor.

After a series of events, David eventually named Solomon King. Adonijah fears for his life, runs to the altar, and grabs the beast's horns. (I imagine Adonijah being chained to a building so the bulldozer doesn't destroy it, as you see in the movies when someone is protesting something.) He stays there until David declares he won't have him killed as long as he does nothing like this again.

Solomon becomes even wealthier than David. God appears to Solomon and tells him he can have anything he wants. He only has to ask. Solomon asks for an understanding heart to discern between good and evil. God says, "I have given you a wise and understanding heart... I have also given you both riches and honor. **If you** (emphasis mine)walk in my ways and keep my commandments." And that is where the problems start.

God requires us to worship him and him only. Israel's continued sin of worshiping idols was her downfall repeatedly. God tells Israel they can avoid that by not mingling or intermarrying with those cultures that worship false gods. Solomon knew this. He knew the teachings. You notice that when Solomon asked for a discerning heart, it was not for himself but for *the people*, meaning the Israelites (I Kings 3:9). Maybe that was his first mistake—just saying.

Solomon does a great job with his new skills. For one superb example, read I Kings 3:16-28. Solomon was flourishing, and his kingdom was expanding. He had wealth that our minds couldn't grasp. Think Jeff Bezos (Amazon's President) on steroids. At this point, Solomon is genuinely grateful and tells God he is going to build God a temple. Everyone is excited, and then Solomon's fall begins.

He conscripted 30,000 Israelites for his projects. The temple is built, and it is magnificent. The temple is dedicated, and Solomon delivers a powerful blessing (I Kings 8:15-60). He ends his blessing with, "Let your heart, therefore, be wholly devoted to the LORD our God, to walk in His statutes and to keep His commandments." God visits Solomon a second time and once again repeats what he told him earlier. There are a lot of 'ifs' (I Kings: 9:5-9).

Do you wonder why God told Solomon the same thing twice? I think it was because God could see the direction Solomon was heading. That amount of fame and money can be dangerous. Wealth can make us believe we are infallible.

In I Kings, chapter eleven, we read of Solomon's further sins, which God gave clear instructions to avoid. We risk losing our connection with God when we intentionally ignore his warnings. But we need only to confess sincerely, and we can begin anew. At this point in Solomon's story, I seriously question his relationship with God.

Solomon collected many wives from heathen nations. I will include these two verses because they are essential to understanding how Solomon went wrong. But as you read them, I want to remind you of James 1: 14:15, which states that *"... each of us is carried away and enticed by our <u>own</u> lust. When that lust takes over, it gives birth to sin."*

1 Kings 11: 9 & 10 state that God was angry with Solomon. God warned him twice about having nothing to do with foreign gods. But Solomon didn't listen.

"For it came about when Solomon was old, his wives turned his heart away after other gods; and his heart is not wholly devoted to the LORD his God... Solomon did evil in the LORD's sight and did not follow the LORD fully..."

The LORD said to Solomon (11-13), "Because you have done this, and you have not kept my covenant and My statutes, which I have commanded you, I will surely tear the kingdom from you and *give it to your servant.*" These are some of the harshest words in the Bible when you consider all God did for Solomon.

Solomon's decline was:

1. Marrying women from idol-worshipping countries.
2. Letting greed take over his life. All his drinking cups and utensils were solid gold. His forty thousand horse stalls directly contradict Deuteronomy 17: 16-17, stating that kings "must not multiply horses nor wives for himself, or his heart might turn away, nor should he greatly multiply his stash of silver and gold."
3. He imposed high taxes on his subjects to pay for

everything.

4. He conscripted labor from his own people. According to I Kings 5:15, there were 80,000 men cutting stones in the mountains and 70,000 men carrying the stones to the building.

Solomon's story ends on a sour note, much like Jonah's. Within weeks of Solomon's death, his empire is permanently destroyed. His father, David, spent forty years consolidating the Israelite empire, and within weeks of Solomon's death, it was permanently destroyed. That's why I call Solomon's more, a lost more. What do we learn from Solomon?

- We are in danger of losing our more when we take a lackadaisical approach to our more. We let little things chip away at us.
- We are in danger of losing our more when we think about ourselves and our wants too much.
- We are in danger of losing our more when we sin. Sin separates us from God; therefore, it separates us from our more.

We lose sight of our more when we quit thinking about our more. Somewhere in Solomon's story, he quit thinking about his purpose. He allowed his thoughts to be diverted by other distractions. While distractions are of significant benefit when struggling with depression and anxiety, they work against us in keeping our more front and central in our lives.

We can read Solomon's story, and once again, we want to yell, "Stop, Solomon! You're going backward." At any point in

Solomon's account, if he had confessed and turned his life around, he could have turned back. We can, too. A thrown-away more is a lost more *only if it remains lost.* Like most lost things, it isn't lost anyway; it's just misplaced.

Therefore, don't despair if you think you've thrown away the more God gave you. It's still there, waiting to be found. We can still use it for God. Maybe it will look different now because it's been a long time since you've dusted it off. But once you do, it will look bright again. You will not have lost in the dark what God gave you in the light.

Solomon's story: Kings 1-11 in the Old Testament.

Ananias and Sapphira

There is another sad story of a lost more, and only a few verses are devoted to it. Acts 5: 1-11 is the only reference to Ananias and Sapphira.

Ananias and Sapphira were a married couple. I am guessing they were pretty wealthy; as verse one states, they sold a piece of property, meaning they probably owned more than one property. Their story is simple. When the time came to pay a tithe, they brought only a portion of the sale as their tithe.

Think of it like this. I don't mean to offend anyone here. Some believe tithing is on net earnings after taxes, 401K distributions, etc., are taken out. But that's not the total amount. Tithing on the gross means tithing on the total amount of your salary. It applies to financial gifts we receive as well. It's not ten percent of the whole unless it's from the initial amount *before* any deductions.

But this is precisely what this couple did. They voluntarily pledged to tithe from *all* the proceeds of the sale to the church. Maybe that's why the scriptures say to be careful about making an oath. I wonder if they received more than they thought they would and figured, "Whoa, I didn't mean that much!"

The fact that they kept some money back isn't what killed them, though. The problem was they lied about it. Ananias was struck dead as soon as he was caught in his lie. "Ananias, why has Satan filled your heart to lie to the Holy Spirit and to keep back some of the price of the land? You have not lied just to human beings; you have lied to God!" He falls over dead right after this question.

Sapphira comes in about three hours later, and when Peter asks her about it, she also lies. Now, wouldn't you think Sapphira might have had a heads-up? Like, why was Peter asking this? Hadn't her husband already been there and taken care of it?

She didn't know what her husband had told them. Should she agree with her husband's statement or tell the truth and possibly get him in trouble? But, of course, he's already dead. She made the wrong decision. She learns her husband has died, but, unlike her husband, she is told ahead of time that she will die. And she does, immediately.

The verse that sums up this story might well be something we need to remember. Verse 11, "And great fear came over the whole church, and over all who heard of these things." Lying to God with our tithes and offerings is serious business. But the church sat up and took notice because of what happened, and a supernatural work began. People that weren't taking God seriously before were taking him seriously now.

Many mores are thrown away due to money and its influence than probably anything else.

Their story: Acts 5:1-5, in the New Testament.

The Rich Young Ruler

The rich young ruler, Matthew 19: 16-26, Mark 10: 17-22, is perhaps the saddest story of all. Jesus is teaching, and a wealthy young man (obviously a trust fund kid) comes up to him and asks, "What good thing can I do to obtain eternal life?" Jesus rebukes him and tells the young man that only one is good, referring to himself. But then he adds, "If you wish to enter into life, keep the commandments." The young man asks which ones, and Jesus responds by quoting the first six commandments. The young man, who senses he's good to go, says, "Hey, I'm keeping all those. Anything else I need to do?" This is where he should have stopped because now Jesus will get right down to the real issue this rich young man has: his wealth.

Jesus says, in essence, "Actually, there is. Go and sell everything you own and give it to the poor." The young man is shocked. Give away everything he owns? He owns a lot! Too much. He can't part with it. Jesus, of course, knew all this, and he also knew the young ruler wanted to hear only what he wanted to hear. Isn't that like all of us at times? We ask God questions but don't want to hear the answer.

Jesus goes on to preach that it is harder for a camel to go through the eye of a needle than it is for a rich man to enter heaven, and the disciples were astonished.

Mark 10:2: "Looking at him, Jesus felt love for him." As far as I know, this is only one of three verses where scripture states that Jesus loved a particular person. John 13:23 mentions the disciple Jesus loved, and John 11:5 says Jesus loved Martha, her sister, and Lazarus. In these last references, Jesus knew these people. He had never met the rich young ruler. So why did Jesus feel a love for him? I am going to suggest something.

I think it was because Jesus saw the more in this young man. He knew what he could become, depending on his response. Have you ever felt drawn to someone while at the same time knowing they were heading for a precipice and hoping you could stop it? I think that was what was happening here.

No scripture indicates the young man might have asked Jesus some questions. I would've thought he would, but he didn't. Perhaps because it was clear Jesus meant exactly what he said. To his credit, though, the young man was sad when he realized he wouldn't do what Jesus asked. You will notice Jesus didn't persuade him or further explain as he sometimes did. Jesus didn't try to convince the young man to change his mind, either. He let him walk away.

As far as we know, the rich young man never found his more. You might wonder how he is an example of a throwaway more, seeing as he never found it.

Except that he did.

He knew Jesus was a great teacher. John 10:17 says, "A man (the rich young ruler) ran up to him and knelt before him and asked him, what must I do to inherit eternal life?" Why would you ask that of a stranger? Why ask the question at all unless your heart had been stirred?

Had he heard of Jesus and his teachings before? Could he have heard Jesus preach before? This young man is someone who knows whom he is talking to.

Jesus didn't ask him to give all his wealth away "just because." God never asks that of anyone. It was so the young man could follow Jesus. His wealth encumbered him. Matthew's account of the reason for giving it all away was to follow Jesus. Matthew 19:23 finishes, "... and follow me." That was it in a nutshell. That was his more, and he threw it away.

A final thought. Many people in the Bible were extremely wealthy, and their wealth was never the problem. God never condemns wealth. What he does condemn is wealth that gets in the way of loving and serving him. If you are a financially wealthy person, be sure you trust God and not your money.

Rich young ruler's story: Matthew 19:16-26 in the New Testament.

TWELVE: DESPERATE MORES

We all feel desperate at times. The following examples are stories of desperation. This first story is one we think we know. But do we?

First of all, who doesn't recognize her name? This woman is plagued by demons, ostracized, made fun of, and yet becomes a follower of Jesus, the only woman in the Bible with her story. One of the few women mentioned in that regard.

Mary Magdalene

Her name appears in three of the gospels. She was one of the first people to receive the news of the resurrection of Jesus.) She followed Joseph of Arimathea and watched as he rolled a stone against the tomb's entrance (Matthew 27:56, 61). She is one of only three people who followed Jesus to the cross and was there when He died. (Mark 15:46-47).

She is often portrayed as a prostitute. Nowhere does the Bible state that. Jesus healed her of seven evil spirits. Some would suggest she had a mental illness. (Luke 8:2). Scripture says little about her, but let's think it through.

Think about the stigma that surrounds the subject of mental illness today. Now, think about a couple of thousand years ago. What do you think it might have been like then? More than likely, Mary was unable to support herself. She was probably homeless, so she likely begged for food. I imagine that when Jesus first saw Mary Magdalene, she was dirty and disheveled.

I am guessing that those who believe Mary was a prostitute might have thought she had no choice but to turn to prostitution if she wanted to eat. I'm not one.

Because of her illness, Mary was likely scorned, made fun of, and avoided. I would imagine she frightened people. And yet, when you think of Mary, do you think of any of that? No. Because you know of her after her encounter with Jesus. There is a series called "The Chosen." It portrays Mary Magdalene as intelligent and thoughtful. I can see where that would be the case.

I was returning something to Amazon the other day via the UPS store. When I went in, I saw a huge, very tall man. He was just standing there. I don't think I've ever seen someone quite that dirty. His clothes were filthy, and you could see his bare stomach. He looked like he hadn't slept in a week. His hair was long, stringy, and dirty. I have no idea why he was in the store except maybe to warm up. I felt so bad for him.

I wondered what his "story" was and knew it had to be sad. No one could look like he did and not have a tragic story. And, yes, I know his story could have been his fault entirely, but that didn't stop me from feeling sorry for him. I didn't know anything about him except for his appearance.

The same would have been true of Mary. People could only know about Mary from how she looked and behaved. They didn't know *her*. Jesus saw who she could be. He saw *her*. Oh, that we would all be seen.

I didn't say or do anything that day. I knew giving him money would be a mistake, although I might have if I'd had my purse with me. I thought about offering to bring him a couple of hamburgers but worried I would embarrass him. I wished I'd had a snack bar or something in my pocket. I could have offered him that.

(As a side note, I have a suggestion. I know someone who keeps small lunch bags in her car with non-perishable goods, specifically those she might see begging on the street corners. It's a great idea.)

Mary went from being an outcast, a possibly mentally ill person, a person scorned and tormented, and became a follower of Jesus all the way to the cross. What a beautiful turn-around story is hers. Is it any wonder she followed Jesus from the beginning to the end and back to the beginning again? After the resurrection, we never hear of Mary again. She appeared only briefly on the pages of history, but when we think of a life turned around, we often think of her. Her story offers hope for all those whose lives have been impacted by mental illness.

In Paul's case, his more was persecuting Christ's followers. If you'd asked him then, he would've said it was his purpose in life. Peter must have thought his more was over when he denied Christ. Mary Magdalene probably thought her more stopped with her healing.

Mary Magdalene's story: Matthew 27:56, 61, Mark 14:40, 47, and John 20: 1,18 in New Testament.

The Woman Bent Over

We know nothing about this woman except that she had been crippled for eighteen years. She can't stand up straight. As the years hurried by, her body has become so bent over she is always looking at the ground. Her story is only told in the gospel of Luke, which makes sense as Luke was a physician, so he would've likely taken a particular interest in a healing like this.

Scholars have speculated she might have had Ankylosing spondylitis, an arthritic inflammation of the vertebrae that can lead to spine curvature. There is still no cure, although there is help now. I know someone with this condition, and while the treatment has come a long way, the prognosis isn't good.

Unable to straighten up, this woman stared at the ground constantly. Jesus saw her and called her over to him. This event happened on the Sabbath in the Tabernacle. "Then he put his hands on her, and immediately she straightened up and was healed." Luke 13:12-14.

Think how hard it must have been for her to even get to the tabernacle to hear Jesus speak. Had she heard of him and his healing powers, or was this what she did every Sabbath? While we don't know, I believe that because the woman was desperate to be healed and went there that day to hear this new young teacher specifically. Did she have any idea she would be healed? Maybe.

We do know this. She didn't like being the way she was. Maybe this teacher she had heard so much about would heal her. Can you imagine how her heart must have leaped when she saw Jesus look right at her and tell her to come forward?

Now, let's stop right here. Jesus could see the woman couldn't get around very well. Right? Why didn't Jesus go to her? What's with asking her to come to him in her condition? Here's my conclusion.

Healing often requires some forward movement on our part. What if Jesus called her, and she said, "I can't." What do you suppose would have happened? There is a reason Jesus had her come to him. It would show her determination and faith if she were the one who had to move. It showed she truly wanted to be healed. She wanted more.

She got up and slowly made it to where Jesus was standing. Like a flower bowed over from a storm now standing straight, she, too, straightens up, standing tall. The woman praises God. I picture her dancing out of that tabernacle.

Imagine yourself in her shoes.

Feel the dust in your mouth.

The dirt in your eyes

As you crawl through the crowds.

Hear the voices all around you.

Smell the smells.

Feel the shame

See the robe

Touch the robe

Hear the voice

Feel the power

Stand up and WALK

Her story: Luke 13:10-13 in the New Testament.

The Man Whose Son Was Dying

Where our children are concerned, if they are ill, we will do anything, pay anything to get them well. We'll spend our savings, sell our house, do anything. What if you knew a miracle worker was in town? I bet you'd do what this man did in our following example.

When the boy's father, a high government official stationed in Galilee, heard this healer had come to town, he went to Jesus and begged him to heal his son. His son was back in Capernaum, a town about sixteen miles away.

"Sir, he is close to dying. We have tried everything. Please, please come and see him."

Jesus *doesn't* go. Can you imagine how crestfallen this father must have been? Why wouldn't he come? What kind of person is this? He's certainly not the miracle worker Peter was led to believe.

All these thoughts, probably some angry ones, circled in this man's head. They had to be. But then Jesus said, "Go, your son will live."

Now, here's where the story gets good, but first...

This father took Jesus at his word. Would you? This man believed and quickly started to head home. Before he could even get there, his servants met him with the news that his son was living and doing much better. He was going to be OK. Now, here's the good part.

The man asked the servant, "When did this happen?"

The Bible is amazingly precise here because the servant replies, "Yesterday, at one in the afternoon, the fever left him."

John 4:53, "Then the father realized this was the exact time Jesus had said to him, "Your son will live." The man's whole household became believers because of this.

This father was desperate, as we all are at one time or another. At some point, we are all desperate for emotional, relational, spiritual, or physical healing.

Keep this thought in your head. If you have asked for healing, maybe it's already begun. Hang on to that hope because there is no reason not to.

Father's story: John, 4:43-54 in the New Testament.

THIRTEEN: LITTLE-KNOWN MORES

Most of these occurred as isolated events. Two of these examples, Ehud and Jael, occurred during times of battle and upheaval. While their mores seem too bloodthirsty, one must remember that this was during a period when the nation of Israel was threatened. Their survival was paramount.

A caveat here. God never instructs anyone to commit murder. These were very specific times and for very specific reasons.

THIRTEEN: LITTLE KNOWN MORES

Ehud

Most people have never heard of Ehud, yet the Israelites would not have been freed from the evil Eglon had it not been for him. His more was far-reaching.

Judges, chapter three tells his story. Israel was under the oppressive rule of Eglon, the king of Moab. The Israelites cried out for deliverance. God sent a man called Ehud, who so happened to carry a sword that was a foot and a half long. His mission was to assassinate the king. Here's what happened.

Ehud told the servants he had a secret message for the king. The servants bought it and left him all alone with the king. The "secret" message was the sword he brought, which he quickly stabbed into the grossly overweight king. Can you see why God picked him? He needed someone with a very long sword to get past all the fat. He made a quick getaway and then led Israel in conquering the Moabites.

Ehud's story: Judges: 3: 15, 21 in Old Testament.

Jethro

Jethro was Moses' father-in-law. In Exodus 18, Moses is overwhelmed because all the Israelites brought all their problems to Moses only, big or small. Moses has way too much on his plate, but he doesn't see it. Jethro does and offers his son-in-law some sage advice.

He suggests that Moses divide his tasks among other leaders and delegate some responsibilities. This division of duties allowed Moses to concentrate on the more significant issues without getting caught up in trivialities. This leadership structure is still followed today by most businesses and governments.

Jethro's Story: Exodus 4:18; 18:1-12 In Old Testament.

Jael

Jael was quite the woman. Judges 4:2 tells her story. Commander Sisera, an evil man, was in charge of Jabin's army. He runs away during a battle and ends up at Jael's tent because her husband and Sisera are at peace with each other. Jael beckons him inside and tells Sisera he will be protected there.

Sisera was exhausted, and after drinking some milk, he fell fast asleep. While he slept, Jael grabbed a tent peg and drove it through his forehead and into the ground! He never saw it coming. The Israelites defeated Jabin's army that same day.

Deborah, the female commander of the army, sang a song that day, and Jael's name is included. The stanza about Jael is, in my opinion, funny. You might want to read it.

Jael's story: Judges 4:2, 17-21, 5:24-27 in Old Testament.

Jabez

Jabez is only mentioned in a few verses in scripture and is known for his "Prayer of Jabez." This simple prayer became the basis for a best-selling devotional book. It's one sentence long, and yet it is so powerful.

Jabez called upon the God of Israel, saying, "Oh, that you would bless me and enlarge my border, and that your hand might be with me, and that you would keep me from harm so that it might not bring me pain." And God granted what he wished.

While these are little-known mores, they were anything but when they occurred. Nations were defeated. Victories won because of these little-known heroes.

Jabez's prayer: I Chronicles 4:10 in the Old Testament.

Anne Frank

Why would I choose Anne Frank as a little-known more when she is very well-known? Because before she was famous, she wasn't. When she died, she was an obscure young woman who was unknown and forgettable, one of the millions.

But what an inspiration she is to those who sometimes think they are unseen and unknown.

Anne Frank. Thirteen-year-old Anne Frank feared for her life while hiding from the Nazis in a secret room for over two years! However, she and her family were discovered and sent to

Auschwitz's death camp. Her father was the only survivor, and it was through him that her diaries were published.

Anne never knew when she kept a diary that her more would live beyond her young life, and she would become an example to people worldwide to this day. Your more may be like that, hidden in obscurity until God chooses it to be revealed.

A child or grandchild who has lost their way may someday remember words of insight from a parent or grandparent that will turn their lives around. Or maybe a dairy.

We think we know our future but haven't a clue. Only God knows our future and the more he has for you. I don't want to come across as a Pollyanna who always sees the bright side of things. That's not me. I can be as negative as the next person.

Growing up, I was often called "Rebecca of Sunnybrook Farm," meaning I always appeared cheerful. I used it as a smokescreen to survive. Perhaps I grew into my name. I'm not sure. But when I say your past doesn't have to defeat you, it comes from the experience of someone whose past could have but didn't. You'll have to believe me about that one.

FOURTEEN UNWORTHY MORES

As I was finishing this book, I realized there was a final category I wanted to cover. I didn't want to call it an unworthy more because that feels so off-putting and demeaning. But when God calls you to something, a more, a purpose, or a mission, it has nothing to do with our worthiness. You might say, "I'm not worthy of a mission." But I know when I express a concern like that, I don't like people only to reassure me. I want them to listen to me and hear my doubts. And I want some concrete help. I want to listen to you. So, let's look at the reasons you might feel that way.

If you're anything like me, you are ashamed of some things in your past. You feel unworthy. I certainly feel unworthy at times. Our past mistakes don't even have to be anything significant, although, of course, they might be. But it doesn't make you unworthy. It doesn't make me unworthy. What it makes us is the need for a Savior.

Alice Walker

A few years ago, I went to a seminar that featured a woman who had been in prison for years for selling drugs. In her case, it was a minor infraction, but she served lengthy prison time anyway. I'm sure at one point, she figured her life was over. She might pick up a book like this and think, "Yeah, right. Me? A more. I don't think so." Except this woman didn't do that.

Instead, she took classes in prison and earned her college degree; while doing that, she counseled women in the same prison. Kim Kardashian learned of her story and fought for her, and she was released after serving twenty-one years. Since then, she has become an advocate for prison reform. She travels the country with her message and has written a book about her story. Her name is Alice Marie Johnson.

I'm sure this woman never dreamed she was worthy of more. But she was and has made a difference in the lives of hundreds of women.

What about serious crimes? Is there a more for a criminal? I can think of one criminal dying on a cross beside Jesus when he found his. (Luke 23: 39-43) Jesus taught through this example that anyone can be redeemed. And if anyone can be redeemed, anyone can have a more. Our pasts might well affect the kind of more we might be limited to, but remember, a more is a more. Isn't that what the Bible is all about?

I would imagine that anyone who has served time in prison often feels unworthy of any kind of more, much less the more to which I refer in this book. Anyone who has been abused for years often feels unworthy. And let's face it, aren't there days we all feel that way? Feelings of unworthiness might be the biggest hurdle one has to overcome to reach for their "more." This is the enemy's plan. He knows we won't reach for more if he can keep us feeling unworthy. Don't give Satan that opportunity.

You are probably not a big offender. You're just someone who made mistakes. You've just done some things in your past that haunt you. If you've asked for forgiveness, it isn't your past that's haunting you; it's *you* haunting you.

Besides, what good is a person curled up in a corner beating themselves up any good to anyone? Only one person would have you stay in a fetal position, and he's the father of lies. *As long as Satan can keep you feeling unworthy, he knows you are useless to God but very useful to him.*

I can hear it now, "But you don't know what I've done." I reply, "You don't know what *I've* done either." Even as I write this book, I am reminded of past mistakes. Sometimes, they weigh heavy on my heart. Sometimes, my past wrongs creep up on me, and my guilt chastises me, "Who do you think you are writing a book?" But then I remind myself that I know who I am—a child of the king, a *forgiven* child of the king.

Yes, our mistakes have consequences. That's life. But that doesn't mean we can't have a more. Our past might become our more because our unique story will reverberate with many. Like with the apostle Paul. When he wrote we are new creatures in Christ, don't you think his hearers thought to themselves, "Now, there's a man who knows what he's talking about!"

No forgiven person is unworthy of a more, a purpose, a mission, or a call. God will give a more to anyone with a willing heart.

But here's what often happens. Sometimes, we use our past as an excuse not to move forward. We've gotten comfortable with our guilt. It's given us many excuses to avoid trying. And besides, it's so much easier to reach higher when you are already on the ladder. But a person in a pit has a long way to climb even to see the light!

I remember struggling with severe depression and wanting to give up, much less think about a more. I had all I could do to get through the day, and if I had seen a book with this title, I would've bought it. But I didn't, so I wrote it.

I had people in my life who saw my more long before I did. (And, yes, that's possible.) I didn't believe them, but their encouragement must have stayed with me because now I've written my second book.

Here's a beautiful quotation I want you to have and put it up somewhere. *"What a wonderful thought it is to think that some of the best events in our lives haven't even happened yet."* Do you know who wrote that?

Anne Frank.

FIFTEEN: QUIET MORES

A quiet more piggybacks off a little-known more. Because these mores are quiet mores, they are often overlooked. These people will probably not have their stories told generations later because theirs isn't a story with a beginning and an end, as much as a continual pouring out. Yet, these mores are equally important and might have a more significant impact than is readily apparent. Let me share some examples.

- What about the person who has decided their more is to make life easier for retail store clerks? That person might make it a habit of straightening up a stack of sweaters because she sees a clerk looking tired. This action might seem temporary, but this person is probably always trying to make things easier for others. That's their more, their calling, their mission. To make things easier for everyone they meet.

- Or maybe the teacher who has decided the cleaning staff has been working overtime, so he picks up the papers off the floor. Or the teacher who tutors anyone who needs her help for free.

- The visitor in the hospital sees a pitcher of water that needs filling and fills it herself. Or the visitor who speaks encouraging words to the nurses and cleaning staff. Maybe they bring baked goods on occasion to treat the staff. They recognize the hard work it takes to work in a hospital. Maybe they drop in on other

patients they've come to know.
- The neighbor who snowplows a driveway anonymously.
- The neighbor who, when on their walk, makes it a habit to return empty garbage cans to the house.
- The person who always stops to talk to an elderly neighbor and doesn't brush them off.
- The person who anonymously pays for a child's trip to camp.
- The person who gives consistently to charities with no recognition.
- The person who anonymously pays for someone's dinner.
- The person who gives up a plane seat so a family can sit together.
- The person who sends flowers every year to brighten a widow's day on the anniversary day of her husband's passing.

Indeed, we hear news stories all the time about a waitress receiving a big tip or a large gift, like a car. These are all examples of quiet mores.

A quiet more is only quiet on earth. Heaven rejoices when anyone sees a need and fills it.

These people have probably never even thought about these acts as their purpose, or as I have been calling it, their more. That's one of the aims of this book, to help people not only discover a new more perhaps, but to recognize when they already have one.

Remember, a more is intentional. When you call it your more, it opens up many possibilities.

SIXTEEN: FINAL THOUGHTS

I've done my best. I've categorized the mores and given you examples and encouraged you to look for yours. Some of you are already accomplishing your more, your purpose, your destiny, your mission, whatever you want to call it.

But some of you are asking, "I get what you're saying, Rebecca, but how do I go about finding my more?" The final chapter gives some practical steps.

I'm one of those people who love learning. I like lists. (I even just bought a book with that title.) I like bullet points. It's just who I am. And I especially like it when an author gets right down to the nitty-gritty with how-tos. I'm all about the how-tos. So, that's what I'm going to do now. (Apparently, writing a book with a self-help section will be my schtick because I've used them with every non-fiction thus far.) But before we go there, let me remind you of some salient points. Here come the bullet points I'm so fond of.

- We all have a more.
- More is a Biblical concept and can be called a mission, purpose, or calling.
- God has called each of us to some special more only we can accomplish.
- Don't dismiss the gifts you have as too small or too unimportant.
- Our mores fit under the umbrella of our spiritual gifts, and everyone has at least one.

- Mores can change over time.
- Mores run the gamut from public to almost unknown.

EVERYONE HAS A MORE.

SEVENTEEN: PRACTICAL STEPS

Here's a short recap in case you skipped to the end. Some of what you read here is redundant. I included it anyway because I know many people jump right to the self-help portion of a book first, and I wanted to make sure you got the important stuff here as well.

My husband and I were on our daily walk. I had been thinking about this concept of more as something beyond purpose, the word 'more' being more straightforward to understand. However, I almost went back to purpose because, as I wrote earlier, editing programs do not like using an adjective as a noun. But I just couldn't go there.

Plus, more is a positive-sounding word and not so laden with the heaviness of words like purpose, destiny, or mission. I asked my husband if he'd ever thought about his purpose in life, having not sprung my concept of "more" on him. His answer was simple. "My purpose is to love God, care for my family, and do it all the best I know how." That's his purpose. He is content with that. And, I should add, he does a great job in all those areas.

Then I asked him, "What is your passion?" I was sure I knew but was curious about what he would say. He replied, "You, the kids and grandkids, and fly-fishing."

Yep, I knew that, too.

My husband is one of those rare individuals whose purpose and passions have always been clear to him. However, he isn't stagnant just because he already knows his purpose, and so he continues to seek God's daily direction. Knowing your purpose doesn't mean you don't keep growing in your faith. He understood where I was going with this, which is good because he is my sounding board for all things spiritual.

He started where we should all start, with the greatest commandment. He got that right, and the rest unfolds for him as he lives his life. But what about those who struggle to define their purpose or passion, their "more," as I call it? I think the minute we ask ourselves if there is a more God is asking of us, we are halfway there.

If we wonder if God has called us to something more, it's because He has. That questioning in our mind is the whisper of the Holy Spirit; otherwise, we wouldn't think about it. It's a deep sense in our hearts that something more is required of us. It might well be something we enjoy doing, but now God calls us to make it our more. But now, God calls us to use those abilities uniquely for his kingdom. It will align with our innate talents and skills, although perhaps yet undiscovered. It will line up with our spiritual gifts.

But does everyone feel that urging for more? Not necessarily. Some may have already found theirs. For another, this might be something they simply never considered. Hopefully, this book at least gets readers to think about the concept of more. But if someone feels there *is* more, there probably is. Some people might feel they are already living their more.

But because a person feels there *is* more for them doesn't make them special. It makes them responsible. "To whom much is given, much is required." (Luke 12:48.) It means that God has called them to go beyond where they are currently. He has a mission for them that only they can accomplish. And it is one that perfectly aligns with their gifts, talents, and season of life. The more is different for each of us; because it is, we should avoid comparing our more with someone else's.

I have been called to write. You would think blogging for about five years would have been a clue. You would have thought leading Bible studies or sharing my faith, which all meant using words, would have been my sign. Deep down, I knew I should write to publish, but frankly, I was scared to pursue it. I still am. I am simply *doing it afraid.*

But a writer isn't someone special because they write. Artists aren't special because they paint. Contractors aren't special because they build. It just means they have found their "more" and are pursuing it. In Christian circles, ministers aren't special because they preach. Bible teachers aren't special because they teach. Choir directors aren't special because they lead the choir. We admire them and support them, but at the same time, we don't elevate them. They are simply doing what God has called them to do. It garners no more adulation than what God has called you to do because:

Relationship WITH God, not accomplishment FOR God, is what matters.

Consider again the parable about the three servants who were individually given various amounts of money by their master and what they did with it. The *only* person who received criticism from the master was the one who dug a hole and buried his money. The other servants had each done something different and increased their original investment. Yet no one received commendation because of the *amount* of the increase.

Two of the servants received the same reward. Why the same? They each received the same amount because each was equally faithful in handling what they were given. Let's say you tell your older child to clean his room and your younger child to clean the closet, and they both complete their tasks. Does the older child deserve more credit than the younger child because his task was bigger? Of course not. They've both done what was required. The size of the project made no difference.

In the preceding parable, the money amount wasn't important, only what was done with it. A bit of ability, talent, and hard work can accomplish miracles. We can dig a spiritual hole, hide our gifts, or multiply them many times over. All of us are given something we can share with the world. We will be rewarded depending on how faithfully we use them and not on the results.

How your more is lived out might well change over time. Our lives are ever-evolving. Certainly, when we're busy with a growing family or beginning a career, we probably don't even have the luxury of contemplating anything else. I can just hear it now. "You want me to look for more? What? I have about as much more as I can handle." And yes, career building and taking care of our families is about as more as it can get. It doesn't mean there aren't those who can successfully pursue other endeavors while raising a family or pursuing a career because there are.

If you've known what you are to do and put it on hold and now fear you've missed your opportunity, nothing could be further from the truth. It depends on why it was put on hold. Read the detoured mores again if you doubt. If the dream has stayed alive in you, it can only mean you are to investigate all the possibilities in your current season of life.

Besides, there are countless stories of people who've put their dreams or mores on hold for a long time, only to embrace them later with great success. Sometimes, they didn't have a choice but to delay; sometimes, they did. If they're still on the shelf, they can be picked up, dusted off, and pursued again. There isn't an expiration date on a call God has given you.

Don't ever let your doubt rob you of your dreams. They're alive in you for a reason. Ecclesiastes 3:1: "To everything, there is a season and a time to every purpose under the heaven."

Even if you know you are doing what God has called you to and you are living your more, please keep reading anyway. You might find these steps helpful for yourself down the road or for someone else.

The following seven tips might seem to have nothing to do with your more, but they have *everything* to do with it. But remember, the examples I used in the book's first half occurred during ancient Bible times. While they were people like us, our lives look very different now. We will not likely experience a burning bush or be struck blind on the road. We live in a twenty-first-century world, not an ancient one. Our more will most likely appear while we take one ordinary step after another. So, where does our journey begin?

It begins with love.

ONE: LOVE

We begin where my husband did with the first and greatest commandment.

All followers of Christ share the same common purpose, as stated in Deuteronomy 6:5: "You shall love the Lord God with all your heart, with all your soul, and with all your strength." The New Testament references add, "love our neighbor as ourselves." Luke 10:27 states it best "... you shall love the LORD your God with all your heart, and with all your soul, and with all your strength and with all your mind and your neighbor as yourself." (Jesus adds the word 'mind'),

It's not called the first and greatest for nothing. Everything else we do builds on this one particular commandment. We cannot hear the voice of God revealing our more if we are not living this commandment to the best of our ability. Any more that isn't first firmly established on this commandment is a more we've invented.

If you only take away one thought from this page, take this one:

If we keep the first and great commandment, our more will be revealed. But if we aren't living out this commandment in every part of our lives, there's a good chance we will never find it, much less pursue it.

Remember, the more I am writing about is the more that originates from God. It is while engaging in everyday activities that our more emerges. I am explicitly addressing mores in the spiritual realm, which are only accomplished through God's direction.

Let's consider these concepts.

Be open to new experiences.

It's easier to love when you open yourself to new people and new experiences. People are always surprised to learn that I am uncomfortable in small groups. I can teach a roomful of women, but three or four couples, and I'm terrified. I like teaching the Bible but don't like being *in* a Bible study with a small group of people. I'm great one-on-one and with large groups but easily intimidated in a small group. In other words, I have control issues.

My first book was written because I stepped out of my comfort zone one summer evening and attended a Bible study in our new church. I didn't know anybody. Opening those heavy church doors and walking inside was scary, and I almost didn't walk into the room. Wouldn't you know it? The tables in the back were full of people like me who don't like to sit in front, but as God would have it, that's where I ended up.

It was in that Bible study I first knew I was supposed to write a book. It was a combination of what the Bible teacher said, what the woman on the video said (it was Beth Moore), and the discussion at our table that all worked together that I found my more. Had I not stepped outside my comfortable place, I wouldn't have. Everything changed for me that night.

Don't be afraid to try something new; put your fear aside

(which will be discussed later) because it might be when you walk through that door, everything changes for you, too.

Treat people like you want to be treated.

How do you want to be treated? Well, then treat others that way. It's not rocket science. Loving our neighbor is much more complicated now. We live further apart. Depending on where we live, we might never even see our neighbors. Both men and women work outside the home. Our lives are hectic. There aren't many "neighborhoods' as we used to think of them.

Also, people are just not as nice. Right? I mean, how did this even happen? I know one of the reasons. Politics. No matter what side of the aisle you sit on. But why? Another reason? Talking heads, meaning those who host various cable shows, all of them. Why can't they give a compliment when needed or say something nice about someone whose views are different? Is it really that hard?

Because of this pervasive fog of meanness, making it a point to interact with people is even more critical. It doesn't mean you walk up to a perfect stranger and say, "Hey, you want to interact?" But most of us go about our day, ignoring the person in the waiting room, the person pumping gas next to us, and the waitress taking our order. These are all occasions to strike up a conversation. Like us, others might be starving for a word or two from someone. Haven't you been there?

Recognizing those around us and talking with them is a way to love. We encounter people every day who might quite literally be wondering if they should even go on. A few words from someone show caring and may change the course of a life. Maybe even save a life. We never know what burdens someone might be carrying. We need to see people as God sees them: worthy of love and worthy of being seen.

Plus, it's amazing how God uses people, sometimes perfect strangers, to speak to us. I've lost track of the number of times I have sensed a God-message from a stranger. Sometimes, we hear strangers best because there is no relationship muddling up the message. If God can speak through a donkey, he can certainly speak through a stranger.

But don't have a misguided sense of what loving your neighbor means. Too many times, we think love is only an emotion. Certainly, it is that, but it's much more than that. Love is action. Jesus said the same thing when he said we should treat our neighbor like we want to be treated. We all know words are cheap and often insincere. Studies have shown that we remember what people do for us much longer than we remember what they say. Unless, of course, they are harsh words. Those we remember forever.

Read how Jesus responded to the people he encountered. When he met hate, he addressed it severely. Jesus wasn't always gentle with his words or his actions, either. He delivered love in uncomfortable ways at times. When we genuinely love people, there will be times when we will have to speak honestly. When someone like the rich young ruler asks a question, we must be as honest as Jesus was and then let it go.

However, loving others doesn't mean we put ourselves in

harm's way. We don't have to be, nor should we be, anyone's rug to walk on. Start with love, and your more will emerge.

But loving God means accepting his love for us, and we do that by loving ourselves.

Love yourself.

"Love the LORD your God with all your heart, all your soul, all your mind and all your strength and your neighbor as yourself." (Mark 12:30)

Most people don't read this entire verse; thus, they misunderstand its full meaning. Yes, it means treating your neighbor how you want to be treated, but it also means loving yourself. What? Isn't that a bit narcissistic?

Not at all.

"As yourself" means you love your neighbor as much as you love yourself. This statement from Christ tells me that God expects us to love ourselves. You've all heard the saying, "You can't love someone else until you love yourself first." That's another way of rephrasing "love your *neighbor as yourself." It is one hundred percent true.*

A good analogy is when you hit turbulent skies on a flight, and the facemasks come down; what are you told to do first? Put it on yourself! Why? Because first of all, putting a mask on someone else will probably take longer and you may not even be able to do it because you are not fully oxygenated yourself. Now you're both in trouble. But putting it on yourself is faster, and you are clear-headed enough to help someone else.

Show me someone who has difficulty getting along with people, and I'll show you someone who doesn't like themselves very much, not to mention love themselves. Every evil act man commits stems from not feeling loved. And when people don't feel loved, they generally can't love themselves. Wouldn't you agree that you know many people who don't like themselves very much? They are almost always disagreeable, short-tempered, self-centered, and egotistic.

Loving ourselves almost guarantees we won't be self-centered or selfish. We won't have a big ego. These qualities don't exist in someone who loves themselves. So, how do we love ourselves without spilling over into egocentricity?

We love ourselves because God does. As Christians, we love ourselves because God first loved us. If he loves us, how can we not love ourselves? And how do you treat a person you love? With kindness, tough love, and encouragement. We do nice things for someone we love, so we should do nice things for ourselves.

However, it is also true that if we love someone, we are honest with them. We're not afraid to have that talk if necessary. That means we are willing to have that hard talk with ourselves. Loving ourselves means demonstrating the very attributes of love, as stated in I Corinthians 13.

Loving ourselves means we place a value on our time as well. We learn to say no graciously when necessary. We also learn to say yes graciously.

Loving ourselves means we watch the words we use in our heads to describe ourselves. We shouldn't label ourselves as stupid or incompetent when we make mistakes. We should give ourselves room to become who we are, pursue our dreams, and use our creativity however we choose.

Next, we have to live our lives.

TWO: LIVE

I don't know where Christians came up with the idea that they are to live restrictive, constraining, and little lives. Or why they think they should constantly beat their fists against a wall, yelling 'Mea culpa, Mea culpa.

I often wonder how a down-in-the-mouth Christian attracts anyone to Christ. We are to emit a sweet fragrance to those around us. Smelling like a bunch of rotten potatoes isn't going to draw anyone to Christ. Besides, we can be salty and sweet at the same time. Attractive Christians aren't mealy-mouthed. One of the ways we are attractive is when people see our authenticity. And we don't sugarcoat our struggles. We don't pretend to be something we're not. At the same time, we don't act like those with no hope. An attractive Christian is known for their love, integrity, and honesty.

Sometimes, we try to live someone else's life, not our own.

Be real.

That means being honest with ourselves about who we really are. Know what you like and don't like. It's like pretending to like apple pie when your favorite is lemon meringue. (I love them both.) It's about personal honesty. We need to walk through our day being honest with ourselves about everything.

I didn't say everyone has to know about it, though. No one wants that much information about anyone. Don't you sometimes wish people on Facebook would keep a few more things to themselves?

I used to be one of those who had to devise an excuse for every no I spoke. "No, I can't do that because..." and then list a thousand reasons why. I answer, "No, I won't be able to help with that," in response to a request. Now, I don't offer any made-up excuses. I don't say I can't unless that's true. I say, "Sorry, I won't be able to help you with that." If I'm asked why, I repeat my response. Our no should be accepted without further explanation, although obviously, there are exceptions. As long as we are kind, we don't need to offer an exclamation to make someone else feel comfortable.

When you think about it, doesn't it seem that when you are the most real with yourself, you feel the most real with God? It makes perfect sense. We often carry over our behaviors with others into our relationship with our Father. If we are insincere with others, we are likely to be insincere with him as well. When there are no pretenses between God and us, we can hear him best. If there is one relationship where total honesty and transparency are paramount, it's this one.

Personal integrity

Living our life is having personal integrity in all areas, especially prayer. We need to be ourselves in our quiet time with God. Many people use formal words with God. They don't even sound like themselves. Yet, there is probably a danger of being too casual. After all, God is a holy God, and so there is something to be said for addressing him that way. At the same time, he is our father. When praying, be consistent with who you are, and remember you are talking with the creator of the universe.

Vulnerability

For me, it isn't about the words as much as my vulnerability. We should be vulnerable with God, willing to speak from our hearts, and willing to speak the truth. If we're mad at someone, is it so wrong to tell God that? "Lord, I'm so mad at (their name.)." Our all-knowing Father knows it anyway. Right? In one of his imprecatory Psalms, Psalm 35, David expresses anger and much more. Besides, how can God help us deal with negative emotions like anger if we don't admit it? And what about depression and anxiety? We need to be honest about our feelings in prayer. How can the Holy Spirit minister to us if we're not open?

I love those times when I can sit, soak in God's word, and reflect. But our God isn't limited to those times, and I find God shows up most when I'm simply going about my day. It feels more like we're a team during those times. He sits beside me while I type; he stands beside me when putzing in the kitchen. Sometimes, when I try to reflect, I concentrate too much. Does that resonate with you? Haven't you found it to be true? I'm more open to the Holy Spirit when I don't work so hard at it and when I routinely go about my day.

I picture Jesus going about his days when no one was around and doing the most mundane things as he walked, like maybe picking up a stone and rubbing it between his fingers. I picture him praying, but I also imagine him chipping away at a rock, fashioning some bird or animal. Or cleaning up his toolbox. We forget that Jesus was fully human, and he, too, might well have found he communicated better with his father when he lived a routine day.

By the way, I love using stones and rocks as decorative pieces because they remind me of The Fourth Chapter Of Joshua I Mentioned Earlier. How About Peter, James, And John? Did They Find fishing a form of meditation for them?

Life is not one-dimensional.

As I write, I am living my life as usual. God is as apt to show up when I'm sorting clothes or organizing a drawer as he is when I'm praying. I often think of something I want to blog about or write about while doing the most routine tasks. Joyce Meyer, author and speaker, shares how she was vacuuming when she realized she was to enter full-time ministry.

Looking for God to show up

The disciples were going about their business when Jesus found them. I can't think of anyone in the Old or New Testament sitting somewhere examining their navels in deep contemplation when God showed up and called them to a mission. Moses and David were tending sheep, a mundane job, when they learned about their more. Paul was on the road to Damascus. God shows up where we are, whether on our knees in the dirt or on our knees in prayer. Besides, if he waited around for most of us to seek him, his followers would be in short supply.

We need to live our lives while always looking for God to show up. To wait around breathless for a particular "leading" can be fruitless.

We need to take a deep breath, get on with living, and trust that if we listen, God will direct us to our more. We continue the heavy lifting of prayer and Bible study and trust that it will all be fruitful. We go about our ordinary days in ordinary ways and watch for an extraordinary God to show up.

Freedom in Christ means we are free to think big and dream big because we love a God who can do more than we can think or even imagine. (Ephesians 3:20.) It's the strangest thing, but just by living our lives, our more often emerges.

We needn't frustrate ourselves in this search. Our more will show up as we follow Christ daily, continue our routines, and pray and study our Bibles. I've found that when I look for something too hard, I seldom find it.

The next lesson is to leave.

THREE: LEAVE

I used to wonder why I had the childhood I had. For what purpose could that possibly have served? I would have preferred something much different.

But without my past, I could not write about depression and anxiety from personal experience. Without my personal history, I couldn't write about my frequent companion, fear. My background well equips me for writing about mental health, mostly because I've lived through depression and anxiety and emerged as somewhat normal. Like everybody else, I still occasionally struggle with some down moods, but depression is definitely in the rearview mirror.

I learned what I could from my past, and now I look to the future. If I were still dwelling on the pain and dysfunction, I couldn't possibly hear God's voice.

Refuse to let your past determine your future. You are not chained to your past unless you choose to be.

Besides, like so many, my past has made me who I am today. I don't hold the trauma of my childhood against anyone. I never did. I forgave my parents because God forgave me, and because of that, we forged good relationships. When my parents died, I grieved their loss deeply, as though the past *had* been entirely different.

It's all about emptying your suitcase. Here's what it means.

Empty your suitcase.

First of all, you can only empty *your* suitcase. You can't empty anyone's suitcase but yours. Think of someone you know. You see them dragging heavy, oversized suitcases behind them, and you so want to help them unload them. *"Here, let me help with that,"* you might offer. You continue, *"Let's get rid of that anger you've held on to for so long. How about those memories of the past? And, while we're at it, let's throw out those hateful words you're hanging on to."* But they refuse. They're not there yet. They're more comfortable carrying it around with them, and they don't know what they'd do without a packed suitcase. Nope, we can't empty anyone's suitcase but our own, and no one can do it for us either.

And the thing about the suitcase is that you might not have put all the garbage in there. Other people may have added a few things; no, other people *have* added a few things. Maybe most of your suitcase is like that, filled with things other people have done to you. But you know what? You're still the only one that can empty it. You have a choice. You can carry around all that extra baggage, or you can empty it. It's unfair, but fairness has nothing to do with it. You're the one lugging around a heavy suitcase.

Our Father's love

While writing this chapter, I took a break to finish the morning's Bible study. It was right after I wrote the previous paragraph. As I prayed, I found myself thinking this:

"Nothing my parents (or anyone else for that matter) did or

didn't do got in the way of my love for them, just like nothing I do or don't do gets in the way of the Father's love for me.

That shouldn't have been a revelation for me, but you know how you can know something for years, but suddenly something strikes you differently, and now you know it in the deepest part of yourself? It was like that. Kind of like putting a period on something that I had left unfinished.

And you can say the same thing. Nothing you do or don't do gets in the way of the Father's love for you. What if I *were* still holding on to the past? Would I have been able to write those words? Would I have been able to grasp my Father's love for me? What would my relationship with my parents have looked like? I had been forgiven so much. What else could I do but forgive them?

Pot. Kettle. Black.

As a child, I couldn't have dreamed of the fantastic life I have now. That I would be so deeply loved by a caring and devoted husband. That I would have a wonderful family and great relationships with my grown children. I know so many who don't. I knew nothing about how a good marriage looked or how to be a good parent. Neither did my husband—his past equaled mine and then some.

But we consciously decided to start afresh from the day we were married. Certainly, we made our mistakes. But we managed to carve a beautiful life out of a dream we dreamed, not the reality we had lived. We did that by leaving the past on the church steps. We knew there was more for us, even if we didn't have a clue where to start.

I would never have imagined writing a book, much less two. But as I look back, I realize God has been bringing me to this place of writing books my entire life. There are lessons learned that I have shared with others through various workshops, retreats, and teaching Bible classes. Lessons about being a frightened child, a woman who suffered depression, a woman who found it difficult to be loved, a woman full of anxiety and fear. In a sense, I've been writing books my entire life; I just didn't know it.

The existential question

As my mother was dying, she asked me one day, "What am I here for?" She felt she served no purpose anymore. Her abilities were severely limited because she couldn't cook or do any of the things she usually did for her family. She never considered there could be a different more for her. Caregiving had always been her more, and she had expressed it in various ways over the years. Now, that was gone.

I answered something like, "Mom, I don't know what I'd do without you." Kind of a lame answer, and I wish I had elaborated on that to this day. But her question had hit an existential nerve and prompted that same question in me, "Why am *I* here?"

Why *are* we here? Why are *you* here? All of us have asked ourselves this existential question. When we know our more, it's easier to answer. That's one of the reasons a more is so important. It helps us answer difficult questions.

We should walk closely with God in a broad place of possibilities, not in a place defined for us by our past. To walk in a narrow and restrictive place is only to thwart those possibilities. While the road to heaven may be narrow and the road broad that leads to destruction, there are no such parameters for fulfilling our more.

In this broad place of possibilities, when we live our lives to the fullest, our dreams and passions converge to our "more." Jesus never preached a sermon that suggested we settle for anything less than more. It was always about more love, more forgiveness, more giving, more, more, more. He even told his disciples that they would do more than he had done.

Gratitude

And we need to express gratitude. Not just feel grateful but speak gratefully. The Psalms are full of instructions to praise God out loud and to praise him often. We need to show God our best manners. I think of all the "thank-yous" I speak in a week. There are a lot of them. But how good am I telling God, "Thank you?" How good are you?

When we gratefully live the life God gives us, we see the more God has for us. It's when we are the most receptive to the voice of the Holy Spirit.

I quite often imagine the following scene. You may borrow it.

Boxes

I love boxes. I collect them like other people collect other things. The older the box, the better. It doesn't matter if it's wood, metal, or plastic. I just love boxes. Maybe it's because I find it easy to use boxes in my imaginings. This imagining is one of those.

It's a scene when I meet Jesus for the first time. He is holding a box. The box had my name inscribed on it the minute I was born. (By the way, in my mind, that box is chalk-painted and distressed. The clasp is gold. The inside is lined with black and white buffalo fabric. (I decorated it differently in my first book.) All the spiritual gifts God bestowed on me when I was born are in it. In my dream, when Jesus opens that box, it is empty. I've used up all those gifts. I know my box isn't empty yet, but I want it to be.

Can you imagine God saying to you, "Well done, my good and faithful servant?" I want to come to the end of my days knowing I've used up all the gifts God has given me. I want an empty box.

How about you?

We are never too old, too this or too that, to empty our box.

Opening this particular box means emptying that other box first, your suitcase. The one that holds your past hurts, the one you keep hidden so you can open it when you need an excuse for not going further in your life. The box that enables you to feel sorry for yourself. The box that keeps you fearful. The box that has become your prison.

Empty that box first. Then you can answer my mother's question, "Why am I here?"

Next, listen to the Holy Spirit.

FOUR: LISTEN

The Holy Spirit is always talking to us. He's always revealing the Father and Son to us and often through other people. I can't tell you how frequently I've sought direction about something, and a perfect stranger says something, and I have my answer. Always pay attention to other people's words, whether audibly spoken or written. The Holy Spirit speaks through many vessels. It doesn't matter whether they believe in God or not. God is not limited in that way. God often uses non-believers in believers' lives, as we read earlier in the story of Esther.

Haven't you had a déjà vu experience when something pops up on the internet or a book you're reading, and you immediately think, "Wow, I was just thinking about that." Or you read an author's way of explaining something, and this new explanation resonates with you. You've read these words before, but now the revelation jumps off the page at you. That's the Holy Spirit revealing to you something at just the right time.

You will hear his voice more often when you understand that God speaks by the Holy Spirit through the people you encounter. Throughout the years, I have frequently been encouraged by people who tell me, "You should write a book." And this was long before it was conscious thinking on my part. The Holy Spirit uses people and circumstances to give us a heads-up. We may not know why, but we should always pay attention and file it away in our minds somewhere, which is why journaling is a good idea. It's hard to remember everything.

We think, or at least we wish, that the Spirit's voice will be like in the movies, a booming voice giving crystal clear direction. Or a kind of lightning-strike experience. Wouldn't that be great? I think of Moses and the Apostle Paul when I think of an out-of-the-box appearance by God. Wouldn't we all like a burning bush kind of experience like Moses? I'm not so sure about the Apostle Paul, though. Blindness, even temporary blindness, doesn't appeal much to me.

But we are not doomed because we don't see a fiery bush or hear the audible voice of God. We have God's word, and we have the Holy Spirit.

Start paying attention to the Holy Spirit. If you don't know how, or if this sounds foreign to you, learn about the Trinity. The Trinity means that God the Father, Son, and Holy Spirit are all rolled up into one, each playing a different role. The Holy Spirit directs us daily and prompts us to understand Scripture. Jesus promised the Holy Spirit would become our guide after he ascended into heaven. But the concept of the Holy Spirit might seem a little out there to some people. How do you hear a voice you can't hear, and how do you distinguish that voice from your own?

Distinguishing the Spirit's voice

One of the best books I've read about hearing God is a book by Dallas Willard called *"Hearing God."* It's not an easy book, but it's a great one. There are also some good books by Priscilla Shirer, Joyce Meyer, John Ortberg, and Andy Stanley. On my blog, https://goodthoughtsgoodlives.com, I have a list of recommended books.

But the best way to learn about the Holy Spirit is to steep ourselves in the Bible and prayer. The more we hear his voice, the more we understand how he speaks, and the more we know how he speaks, the more we hear his voice. It's a beautiful circuitous circle. Our ears become sensitized to his slightest whisper, and we hear his voice everywhere.

Prayer

The more the Spirit leads us, the more we learn about ourselves. I pray out loud. I find hearing my own voice and the words I pray reveals a lot to me *about* me and my motives. Very often, words come out of my mouth, and I have no conscious awareness of thinking of the words first. At these times, I know God is using *my* voice to speak to me.

We know Jesus prayed aloud because the disciples heard him pray in the Garden of Gethsemane. If he did on that occasion, he probably always prayed out loud. Praying out loud does a couple of things.

First, it keeps us focused. It's much easier to lose your place and let your mind wander when you pray silently. Second, it allows you to hear your own words. You can hear your whiney or complaining. Hearing the words coming out of our mouths reveals our moods. We might try to cover up some feelings, but they give us away if we listen to our words. Third, praying out loud keeps us honest.

The Spirit prompts us to offer up quick prayers throughout the day. I call them arrow prayers because I quickly shoot them up.

"God, I'm wondering about...."

"God, is this the best use of my time?"

"God, help me find my glasses."

"Lord, I just need a little sign that my prayers for *so and so* are working. It doesn't have to be much, just something so I won't give up." (I don't pray that often, but when I have, God has *always* given me a little word or sign of encouragement.)

Through this constant dialogue empowered by the Spirit, we develop an intimate and ongoing relationship with God.

Next, learn about yourself.

FIVE: LEARN

Most of us never get acquainted with ourselves. We don't know who we are.

So.....who are you?

Ask some questions.

- What do I like to do? (No. Not what you *think* you're supposed to like, but what you *enjoy* doing.)
- What do I love to do more than anything else?
- What do I wish I could do more than anything else?
- What grabs my attention?
- What TV shows do I watch? (For example, if it's cooking shows, you are obviously interested in cooking. Maybe write a cookbook?)
- What movies appeal to me?
- What kind of books do I like to read?
- When I'm in a bookstore, what magazines do I browse? Photography, art, decorating, travel?
- What do I naturally gravitate toward when I have free time?

Ask trusted people in your life what they see as your talents. But remember, a particular talent isn't necessarily your spiritual gift. I've been told I've missed my calling as an interior designer. Nope, I haven't. I enjoy decorating my home and helping others, but that's it.

We have probably heard this next question. What would you

pursue if you knew you couldn't fail? Mine was writing a book, and here I am, fail or not.

God gives each of us spiritual gifts with the underlying talents and abilities to exercise those gifts fully.

All. Of. Us.

Each. Of. Us.

I like to paint. I think God created that desire in me at birth, although it was in the process of living my daily life that I discovered it. It's something I like to do, like decorating. But I know it's not my more. I share those talents with others, but they are not what God has called me to do with my life. I love to write. God created that desire in me, which *is* how I fulfill my spiritual gifts. Writing is my more.

It takes time and practice.

God gives us our interests and some innate talent. But we must develop the skill set. No matter how much innate talent they are born with, every great musician, painter, writer, chef, or quilt maker will tell you they have worked hard to develop their skill. They constantly learn and grow.

No one truly masters their particular area of expertise without hard work. It's an insult to their success to suggest otherwise. Malcolm Gladwell, in his book *Outliers*, says, "The key to achieving true expertise in any skill is simply a matter of practicing, albeit in the correct way, for at least 1,000 hours. So, we need to give homage and credit to those who have succeeded and let their success and hard work spur us on.

Perseverance

However, don't let the hard work deter you. When I started blogging, I wanted to quit every day for a month or two. It was awful. I knew absolutely nothing. I don't know how my blog ever made it past the first layer of the blogosphere.

I had a lot to say and many ideas to write about, but the technical part was way beyond me, and I failed repeatedly. No one I knew blogged, and I didn't know any other bloggers. So, I did the only thing I knew to do. I read and researched everything I could. I felt overwhelmed with all I had to learn, but I knew this was my first step in writing, and I knew God was behind it. It is the steepest learning curve I've encountered thus far in my life.

When I first began painting pictures, not walls, I sat in front of a piece of white paper transfixed in fear. My art teacher leaned over and whispered, "Rebecca, it's only a $3.00 piece of paper." (It's about three times that much now.) I was an awful painter initially, but I kept at it. Whether I'm any good now or not depends solely on the viewer. My first patient in the hospital as a chaplain? You don't want to know how inept I was.

But with all these attempts, I learned a lot about myself. I learned what wasn't important to me, what didn't grab my heart, and what I could easily move on from, like becoming a great cook. It simply wasn't that important to me. Thank goodness, my husband is a forgiving man with simple tastes. Besides, he says I'm an excellent cook.

However, when something *was* important to me, I was like a

dog with a bone; I wouldn't give up. All the trying and failing taught me a lot about myself. God does not just give us our gifts willy-nilly. There is a reason, a more, a purpose for these gifts. We are to be beacons, lights on a hill, and the only way we shine like that is when we are doing what we have been called to do and we embrace and develop our more.

The more we learn who we are, the clearer our more will be and the more likely we will succeed.

But there is something else you need to know and learn about your spiritual gifts. Many make too big of a deal about this, making it seem complicated to figure it out.

It really isn't.

The Bible lists spiritual gifts in different sections, which can be confusing. There is a lot of information online. Check out some reputable ones like Tyndale Publishing, Moody Bible Institute, and Austin Precept.

Next, we must lose something.

.

SIX: LOSE

I can't swim.

Let me repeat. I **cannot** swim. I could as a child. You might be wondering, well, why can't she now? When I was about twelve, I was swimming across a small lake and got caught in the weeds. They started to drag me down, and I almost drowned. I can't remember how I freed myself, but it was terrifying. I'm too afraid even to try now.

Fast forward several years. My husband and I were on vacation and signed up to go snorkeling. I should say my husband signed us up to go snorkeling, and I humored him. There was no way I was jumping off a boat into water over my head.

I put on the snorkeling mask, the lifejacket, and the flippers, again to humor him. The other couple on board dove into the crystal-clear water. My husband patiently waited. I can still feel how hard my heart was beating at that time. To my great surprise, I jumped in. I still can't believe I did that. I can't even tell you what I was thinking at the time. It seemed as though I couldn't *not* jump in.

But I did. Scared to death, I did. Immediately, I realized I could stay afloat with no problem. It was one of the most exhilarating, awe-inspiring, and God-praising experiences I've ever had. The shapes and shades of turquoise, pink, and green tropical fish and the orange coral were breathtakingly indescribably beautiful. I was awestruck at God's creation beneath the surface of the sea.

A few years later, I was asked to go kayaking with friends. I will remind you again. I *CAN'T* swim.

I got into the kayak and shoved off, again my heart beating wildly. I was terrified I would tip over, which would be the end of my kayaking forever. That could be why I've never tipped over. I'm too afraid of drowning, so I work extra hard at staying afloat. The trip was terrific. I've gone kayaking many times since then, but there is still some fear every time.

I'm frightened today as I write. What if I go through all this and no one reads this book?

That brings me to this:

Do it afraid.

Fear is, and I suspect always will be, my nemesis. There are concrete reasons why, and I'm fully aware of what they are. So, I do pretty much everything afraid. When I wrote my first book, especially the publishing part and learning all the various computer programs I had to learn, I think I lived in constant fear. When it was published and in my hands was the first time I breathed.

I know about fear, up close and personal. I also know how God has been my source of strength when I think my fear might consume me.

Do what you believe is your more and do it afraid. Don't wait for the fear to go away. It may never. But it doesn't have to stop you.

I no longer feel I must be *un*afraid (Jumping off that boat settled that for me.) before I attempt something for God. By the way, while the Bible says, "Do not fear" in many places, it never states, "Wait for your fear to be gone before you attempt something." And all those verses about fear never once suggest that your fear will disappear if you go ahead. What they *do* say is to bring your fears to God and go from there.

Fear is normal.

Do you think David didn't have at least a moment of fear facing Goliath?

Honestly, do you think Daniel didn't have a moment of terror when he saw the lions looking like they were about to devour him?

How about Esther when she went uninvited to see the king? Don't you think she feared for her life, knowing that death was the standard punishment for such an act?

Fear is a normal human emotion, which is why so many scripture verses address it. But fear is an emotion, not a fact. Fear is not a predictor of success or failure. An excellent book by Dr. Susan Jeffers titled *Do It Afraid* is a classic. I suggest you read it if fear is as much an obstacle for you as it often is for me.

Let's say you know the more God has for you, but fear squeezes your heart. Don't think about it anymore. The more you think about your fear, the more fear you will feel. Those moments of fear are a path for Satan to sneak in. It's an open door. If he can keep you afraid, he can keep you useless for God, which is his ultimate plan. If you think you've got your more figured out, jump in. If you got it wrong, God will show you, but don't give up until he does.

Don't doubt in the dark (your present fear) what God has revealed to you in the light (when you are not afraid).

Fear as a motivator

Pretty much everything I do, I do it afraid. Fear has been my nemesis my entire life, but fear has also been my motivator. I would rather feel the fear of rejection than I would the fear of not even trying.

I've made fear my motivator. What if you reframed your fear as well? Like many authors, I hate talking about my book, and I'm not too fond of book signings. I just want to write. But it comes with the territory. I don't even try to tell myself I'm not afraid anymore at a book signing. Besides, how do you deny the heart flutters and the dry mouth? You don't. You just grin and bear it and move ahead.

If you can't find a way to make fear your motivator, or if you're not afraid anyway (lucky you), find something else that motivates you. It could be a scripture verse, a motivational saying, a reward, a person, anything.

Don't backtrack.

After you lose your fear, don't look for it again, either. It's interesting how we return to an unhealthy place because we are comfortable there. We know how fear feels. This new freedom is hard to take. But fear will hold you back from embracing your more. I "get" fear. I really do. It's been the monkey on my back my entire life, but I learned to admit it and go ahead despite my fear. Fear is universal anyway. We all fear something.

However, suppose you can't name your fear. In that case, it might be Generalized Anxiety Disorder, which often requires medical intervention, either medication, counseling, or both. That kind of fear is crippling and will get in the way of unleashing your more.

The final step is to leap.

SEVEN: LEAP

This final step is a big one.

It requires motivation. It means looking fear squarely in the face and just doing it. We discussed this in the last chapter.

Get out of your boat!

I love the apostle Peter. I am like him in many ways because I, too, sometimes act before I think. Peter was highly motivated when he stepped out of the boat and onto the water. Yes, he started sinking when he looked down at the waves instead of straight ahead at Jesus. But he walked on water. Let me repeat: *Peter walked on water.* How many of us have done that?

We have to get out of our boat. We don't get out of the boat next to us. We don't get out of our friend's boat. We only have to get out of our boat.

Like Peter, we may start to sink, but all we have to do is reach out to Jesus, and he will keep us from drowning. I almost sank many times when writing the first book. But I learned (because I know me) that I had to walk away and clear my mind when I felt overwhelmed and afraid. I had to distract myself with something else. Like Peter, I tend to notice the wind before I notice the Savior.

Peter didn't hesitate to get out of the boat when Jesus beckoned him. And neither should we. Putting this book out there in public with the fear of people criticizing me or saying, "Who does she think she is?" almost kept me in my boat. But you know what?

I'd rather leap and make a mistake than look back years from now and realize I didn't leap when I could. I'd rather take whatever critical remarks come my way than look into Jesus's face and be asked, "Why didn't you just get out of the boat and write those books? I was right there with you in every word, every sentence, comma, and period."

But to leap means to be motivated.

Motivation

What motivates you? (This is where knowing oneself can make a difference.) If you look at people, you won't get there. You can only look to God. I am a highly motivated person, *except when I'm not*. And that "not" can derail me. Can you imagine writing for months on end in what could be a fruitless exercise? I've had to do that, always remembering that the only audience I am ultimately writing for is God. That is what motivates me. That and this statement I wrote down years ago and just found again. (I have the name of the person who wrote it, Sara Thomas Dougherty, but I have no idea who she is. I couldn't find her anywhere when I searched. Nonetheless, I wanted to give her credit.)

"There is someone out there with a wound in the exact shape of your words."

I love that; it reminds me that we never know how our words can make a difference. It tells me that someone *will* read this book, and my exact words will begin to heal their exact wound.

I wish I could pump up some people with an injection called "The Motivation Immunization." If I did, I would pump it into everyone who needed it, free of charge. Not intelligence, talent, money, or education makes a difference if you don't get out of your boat.

Some of the most intelligent, gifted people I know have missed accomplishing their more because of a lack of motivation. A lack of motivation is just a disguise for fear. People all around us accomplish great things, fear and all.

Did you know many famous people suffer from extreme stage fright? Barbara Streisand, one of the greatest singers of all time, is one such example. Many contemporary actors and singers admit to great fear before stepping out on stage, Christine Bell being one of them. So, how do we know their names? Because they got out of their boat.

Don't be afraid to embrace your 'more' and where it may take you. One of my favorite scriptures and the theme of this book, Ephesians 3:20:

"Now to Him who is able to do far "MORE" abundantly beyond all that we ask or think, according to the power that works within us...." (Emphasis mine)

This section of the book could have been much longer. I certainly had enough material. But there is a reason sometimes to be scarce with one's words. Sometimes, people aren't ready for all the words written on a subject; they can only read the few that get to the point. If a book were published of just the recorded words Jesus spoke in the Bible, it would be a very small book. Jesus didn't use many words but made his point, didn't he?

Finally, ask yourself, "Could there be more? Am I sure I'm using my gifts and ability to their fullest? Am I emptying my box?"

Don't be afraid to pursue that one special purpose, passion, that more, whatever you want to call it. Believe that if you walk close to God, you are assured that he will help you fashion your more for his unique purpose. You may have a lot of work to do. It might not be easy. There may be people who scoff. None of those matters. At all.

I hope you enjoyed this book. If you struggle with mood disorders like depression, anxiety, and general low moods, be sure to read my first book, *Depression Has a Big Voice. Make Yours Bigger!* or follow my blog, https://goodthoughtsgoodlives.com, where I address these issues. You can find it at all online stores, including Apple Books and Smashwords. I would love to have you comment on my blog.

God bless you as you discover all the more God has for you.

THE SEVEN STEPS TO FINDING YOUR MORE

LOVE (God and people)

LIVE (Your life)

LEAVE (The past behind)

LISTEN (To the Holy Spirit)

LEARN (about yourself)

LOSE (Your fear)

LEAP (Into your "more")

'

Don't miss out!

Visit the website below and you can sign up to receive emails whenever REBECCA PLATT publishes a new book. There's no charge and no obligation.

https://books2read.com/r/B-A-NMKR-SUMRC

BOOKS2READ

Connecting independent readers to independent writers.

Did you love *FINDING YOUR MORE*? Then you should read *Depression Has a Big Voice. Make Yours Bigger!*[1] by REBECCA PLATT!

Overcoming Depression and Achieving Victory. This 60-day devotional is packed with supplementary self-help resources to help you overcome depression and emerge victorious. Expanded version.[2]

Depression is a joy-sucking, peace-robbing illness, and it can strike anyone at any time. It is no respecter of gender, ethnicity, education, or socioeconomic status. It is also no respecter of religion. Christians can struggle with depression just like anyone, and that is the demographic targeted in this book.

For too long, the subject of depression in churches has been ignored. Or worse yet, churches adopt the same stigmas

---

1. https://books2read.com/u/47RRq7

2. https://books2read.com/u/47RRq7

surrounding mental health. When was the last time you heard a sermon focusing on depression and the Christian? Even if it is addressed, there is still that unspoken idea that if you were really a good Christian, you would be able to cure it yourself.

Tell that to the great authors and scholars Charles Spurgeon, John Piper, Beth Moore, and John Ortberg. The list is long. Throughout history, great men and women of God have struggled with this illness. It has nothing to do with a lack of faith. We are all wired differently, and certainly, our brains are. Also, past trauma hardwires our brains to respond in different ways, and we might find ourselves more prone to depression and anxiety.

How we think, our language, and our behavior all play a part in either causing an episode or contributing to it. Therefore, lifestyle changes usually need to be examined. Sometimes, medication is needed in the beginning so one can at least find the mental clarity to begin the hard work of battling their depression, but it is not usually a long-term solution.

This devotional supplies much-needed help while a person is recovering from their depression. The sixty days provide insight into the illness with scripture verses and questions to help the reader begin their journey to wholeness. There are a number of appendices with additional "helps".

You do not have to fight this battle alone, and victory is awaiting you. God can bring you to the other side of your illness and equip you to live a more joyful and fulfilling life.

God bless you as you take this journey.

Read more at https://goodthoughtsgoodlives.com.

Also by REBECCA PLATT

Depression Has a Big Voice. Make Yours Bigger!
FINDING YOUR MORE
Deeper

Watch for more at https://goodthoughtsgoodlives.com.

About the Author

Rebecca Platt is a graduate of Grand Valley State University with a major in Psychology. Postgraduate courses: Clinical Pastoral Education.

She is a former Bible teacher and lay counselor. She has conducted retreats and been the guest speaker for numerous conferences. She is currently a full-time author who has written two other nonfiction books: *Depression Has a Big Voice* and *More!*

She also writes fiction novels under the pseudonym Perry Rowe, the first of which is *"The Second Best Christmas."*

She blogs at goodthoughtsgoodlives.com, where she focuses on living a joy-filled life free of depression and anxiety.

She loves writing, reading, Bible study, researching, and all things DIY. She and her husband live in an old farmhouse that they have completely remodeled. Oh, and she is a coffee lover. Read more at https://goodthoughtsgoodlives.com.

www.ingramcontent.com/pod-product-compliance
Lightning Source LLC
Chambersburg PA
CBHW051317130726
47987CB00004B/1843